My War with Vietnam

My War with Vietnam

*A Pilot's Healing Journey
Home from War*

RICHARD W. JELLERSON

Foreword by Todd Mattox

McFarland & Company, Inc., Publishers
Jefferson, North Carolina

ISBN (print) 978-1-4766-9760-4
ISBN (ebook) 978-1-4766-5536-9

LIBRARY OF CONGRESS CATALOGING DATA ARE AVAILABLE

Library of Congress Control Number 2025000574

© 2025 Richard W. Jellerson. All rights reserved

No part of this book may be reproduced or transmitted in any form or by any means, electronic or mechanical, including photocopying or recording, or by any information storage and retrieval system, without permission in writing from the publisher.

Front cover images: author as General Abrams' aircraft commander (credit Paul Mac Michaels author archives); *background* © PorcupenWorks/Shutterstock.

Printed in the United States of America

*McFarland & Company, Inc., Publishers
Box 611, Jefferson, North Carolina 28640
www.mcfarlandpub.com*

Table of Contents

Foreword by Todd Mattox 1
Preface 3
Introduction 5

Army Flight School 21
Vietnam First Tour, Combat Assaults 35
Second Tour, Flying Generals and Movie Stars 89

Thailand 113	France 155
Hong Kong 119	Ireland 159
Lebanon 123	Spain 161
India 129	Africa 163
Australia 135	Pakistan 165
Italy 141	Persia 167
England 143	Iceland 169
Scotland 149	Home 171
Greece 151	

Glossary 187
Index 189

Foreword

BY TODD MATTOX

I had never heard of Pan American Flight 001 when my cousin Richard told me about it. Chances are, neither have you reading this now. From 1947 to the 70s, a ticket on this luxury airliner took you around the world for a year, visiting San Francisco, Honolulu, Hong Kong, Bangkok, Delhi, Beirut, Istanbul, Frankfurt, London, and New York. You could disembark anywhere along the route and stay if you wanted: two days or two months. The flight came through every couple of days, so you could continue the journey at your whim. Far more than a vacation, this offered adventure. For Richard, it became an odyssey of healing.

I didn't really get to know Richard until well into adulthood. He is ten years my senior and our rare family gatherings meant we were aware of each other but didn't know each other well. Growing up, I knew he had been a helicopter pilot in Vietnam. For those who remember that time in our country, our young men came home, not to parades and gratitude for their service, but distrust, sometimes open hostility. In the Civil War PTSD was called "Soldier's Heart," in World War II, "Shell Shock." All wars leave their nightmares. But our Vietnam vets had to suffer their physical and emotional scars in a country that chose not to care about them. I never saw any such Veteran issues with Richard. He was always affable, full of humor, and interested in whatever I was doing. I assumed some guys got

Foreword by Todd Mattox

through the war unscathed. I was well into my fifties before I learned about the harrowing battles and bloodshed that Richard had faced. I learned about it when he told me the story of how he chose to return to America after the war.

He took the long way home. He bought a ticket on Pan Am Flight 001. For the better part of a year, he took his time, explored, hung out, ate, drank, had long conversations, found friends, lovers, and joie de vivre. In that time, through the people whose lives he shared, he reunited with humanity. When he told me the story, I joked that it was *Eat, Pray, Love* meets *Apocalypse Now*. Richard wasn't unscathed by the war, but he took a chance that a trip around the world might get him ready to go home. He didn't know he would find healing.

Preface

This is not a war story. It does address some wartime experiences of mine for context. It is rather a story about the innate kindness and warmth of humanity and the power of human touch. It's about the ability we each have to reach out to those who are accepting and heal open wounds of pain and loss.

This humanity can often be simply shared and offered to another with just a hug, an honest, firm handshake or a squeeze of the shoulder. In its simplest form it might be just a welcome smile from a total stranger.

The healing discussed in this book took me by surprise. At first, I didn't recognize I needed to heal. I expect a reader wouldn't recognize any need either without the insights I've made about flying combat missions in Vietnam. I was never physically wounded. But the psychic wounds from the inhumanity that is war were deep and open.

More open and much deeper than I knew.

My thanks to both Pamela Wheeler and Vivian Callahan. They did read-throughs and made insightful, often powerful suggestions. I want to thank Bill Fortier as well for his diligent edit. Special thanks to Shirley Schulz, my beloved aunt and patron of the arts. Also, thanks is due Tom Lasser for his technical support. I still fly but no longer fly Hueys. He refreshed my memory on the intricacies of emergency procedures for those special aircraft. And thanks to authors Marc Yablonka and Dr. James Delgado for their encouragement and advice.

Preface

My cousin, Todd Mattox, deserves some special thanks. It was over a good single-malt scotch that he, not I, came up with the idea that this journey of mine was a book. An accomplished screenwriter himself, he then functioned as muse, editor, occasional rewriter and often interrogator, leading me to relive the experience. And we grew even closer through the process. Writing about it was like taking that same healthy, healing journey once again.

Introduction

Didn't want to go home yet. Kinda surprised me. It was 1970.

After being an Army helicopter pilot in Vietnam I was sure I'd just want to get back to family and friends, backyard barbeques and Southern California beaches. I had lived in Hawaii for nearly a year. Then a year-long Army flight school and two tours in Vietnam. So, except for one week, I'd been away from home three and a half years. So why didn't I want to go straight home? I was out of the Army.

A civilian again. So why?

Didn't yet recognize I needed healing. Just felt a restlessness and wanderlust I thought I could address by traveling the world. Wanted to get to know other people, visit other cultures and explore this planet. So, instead of going straight back to Los Angeles, family and home, after my second tour, I bought a ticket on Pan American Flight One. This was an amazing concept from the company that pioneered passenger aviation. The ticket was a magic carpet to many countries around the planet.

Between my two tours of duty in Vietnam I was given a month's leave. I took the long way back to the states: Pan American Flight One. The Army bought that first airline ticket for me, part of the deal for my agreeing to return for a second tour in Vietnam. The flight stopped at most of the world's major cities. That first time, though, I had to make the entire trip around the world in one month. The best part and a truly unique innovation was that the ticket was good for an entire year! It allowed you to get off and stay in a country as long

Introduction

as you wanted. Then get back on the next Pan Am Flight One headed west. Spent three weeks of that first trip in England and a couple other wonderful places.

The hound had been blooded, though. There was more going on in me than I understood. I wanted to see this planet. Calcutta, Istanbul, Tehran, Bangkok, Hong Kong, Berlin, London … the world.

Spin the schoolroom globe. I went alone.

A year and a half earlier, mid–December, 1969, Long Binh, Vietnam. It's at least a hundred degrees, likely more. Directly under the focal point of the sun a large amphitheater boils over with thousands of soldiers waiting for the Bob Hope show to begin.

Sweat. Incurable thirst. Dust. Mind-sucking heat, mind-sucking war. Only takes a year of your young life if you survive it. Then years of hesitation to admit you had a part in it. I think very much like being in denial of a drug or alcohol addiction, this only postpones the cure, the healing.

The daily rhythm of this war lies between the poetry and power chords of rock and roll, the guttural cadence of a Huey helicopter and your own pounding heartbeat. These incessant, pagan, and visceral poundings are gone today. They're strangely replaced with swing music and punch lines.

Les Brown and His Band of Renown plays, "Thanks for the Memories." Then, Bob Hope is on stage making jokes.

No, Mr. Hope, it doesn't seem like Christmas with the heat and the smell. Sides don't ache from laughter. Eyes don't seem to fill with joyous tears. The laughter seems somehow strained or caused by something other than humor. But we all know Mr. Hope doesn't have to be here. He hasn't spent Christmas at home since before most of us were born.

And what he's saying is funny. We're just out of practice.

It's probably been months since any of us really laughed at anything. The applause is heavy. We're entertained. Grateful. Mr. Hope is a hero in his own right.

Then, with a wave of his putter … there's silence. Bob says, "Here's what you came to see.... Let's bring out the girls!" They're what we came to see, all right. And before they hit the stage a

Introduction

thousand soldiers detonate into applause, catcalls, hoots and whistles. A thousand man-boys who haven't seen a round-eyed woman in months and months erupt as one.

As boys, we had always taken the presence of women for granted. Many stand and yell, "Bring them on!" We all think, at first, just for our entertainment.

Our pleasure. Our inspection.

Then, suddenly, they're on stage. And they are more beautiful than any of us remembers. They are more graceful, more feminine and more wondrously curved than our tormented night dreams or carefully crafted daydreams remind us.

They are met with silence. Our noise stopped as quickly as it started.

The last irreverent catcall died, stifled on a startled G.I.'s tongue.

The band plays. The girls smile. Without thinking, like returning a yawn, we smile back.

Some of us stare, awed by the reality that there is such a thing as Woman.

We're all brave, scared boys on a forced march to become men. For months, the guys in the infantry have lived with blister-hot steel guns and tanks all day. Then slept fitfully on the same angry metal all night as it cools. Anyone who has seen action here for more than a month is tougher and older inside.

We've worked cynicism into an art form. We are a hard bunch to surprise or impress. Yet we all stand off-balance, open-mouthed.

The enormity of the void of men living without women astounds us. Another surprise we weren't prepared for in our short, young lives. We need them.

And maybe not just sexually, as we imagine constantly.

We live under fire there too, assaulted and oppressed.

Maybe the need is a balancing force, a nurturing partnership. The first glimmering recognition of a grand design and higher purpose to both life and this amazing man-woman thing seeps into our hormone-deluged brains. It's taken their sudden loss and surrogate reappearance months later to teach us something new again.

Introduction

Maybe it isn't just about how they fit into their jeans. Maybe it's how we fit into each other's lives.

With this realization, living through even just one more day in this place becomes desperately more important. Here are new reasons to survive.

You can actually see resolve hardening some eyes and expressions. Most of us in this war haven't lived long enough yet to clearly view the big picture. I'm twenty years old flying Army helicopters. I've heard it said that the average American soldier in this war is a teenager. Hell, my first crew chief was seventeen. Idiot lied about his age just to get here.

All of us had been dropped into a seething emotional tempest. But by nature of our upbringing in America, the only acceptable outlet for emotions here is anger. Other emotions—hell, all the rest are held in check. We couldn't let them out of the maze even if we knew the way.

Be brave. Don't look elsewhere for strength. Be a rock! A soldier! A man! We try. We internalize everything. The ones who can't go nuts and go home early.

It already feels like childhood was just a dream I had once.

I think the dream weakened, began slipping away and ended in a sultry mist the same overcast morning we flew into Fire Support Base Diamond.

Fire support bases were small outposts built to protect sections of the countryside with villages or bridges nearby. They were armed with artillery, Howitzers, and often Special Forces and recon units.

Fire support bases were widely used during the Vietnam War and their purpose was to provide artillery fire support to infantry operating in areas beyond the normal range of support from their own base camps. FSBs follow a number of plans, their shape and construction varying based on the terrain they occupied.

Often, like FSB Diamond, they were star-shaped, allowing for defensive crossfire.

There had been "Human Wall" charges all night long on the little base carved out of the dense jungle. This meant even the big Howitzer cannons were fired zero elevation—at ground level. Fired

Introduction

directly at the charging enemy. There were four hundred dead Viet Cong bodies and body parts flung in a horrific, surreal display in the perimeter wires.

Growing up here is ugly, brutal and fast. We handle it as best we can. But at what cost? I think only time will tell.

In battle we are stoic and brave largely because of peer pressure. None of us have permission from the rest to admit we are scared. Very soon we learn there's no time to be scared here anyway.

There's a weird, esoteric natural bond forged with others in combat. No one reaches out for strength. Strength is offered in the clandestine agreement that we are brothers in arms. We are in this together, counting on each other, trusting one another with our lives, no matter what the hell comes down that pike.

There's a code we acknowledge only in silence. It isn't written down anywhere. Nobody I ever flew with even talked about it. But as a new pilot in-country, the first time you see it in action, you get it. And then you have a decision to make. Accept and embrace it. Or get out of the combat unit.

"Leave no one behind." That's the mantra. It's a promise made to every American going into war in service to their country. The promise is made by our government and means even if you are Missing in Action they will search for you forever.

It's comforting until you understand how it needs be accomplished in war. And how it surfaces in combat. How it impacts you as an individual is more complex and complicated. It becomes an insidious governing dynamic in war affecting decisions and choices you never thought you would make.

Imagine you are only maybe a week or so in Vietnam. Still a copilot. Still learning and in awe of what you see every day. Then one day you come across an extraordinarily intense battle. It's surreal and so abstract from everything you've ever experienced in your life so far, it's unbelievable. Everything you've believed in and held dear just changed forever.

A company of infantry in a jungle clearing are taking extremely heavy fire from the tree lines. The sheer volume of green and white

Introduction

tracers from Russian and Chinese ammunition is intense. Constant. Unending.

The guys on the ground must be surrounded by hundreds of enemy soldiers. A helicopter has been shot down, burning in the clearing. It was a medevac ship. They fly into firefights unarmed to pick up our wounded. But since North Vietnam never signed the Geneva Convention the enemy sees the big red crosses on the cargo doors and nose only as excellent targets. Can't see survivors or crew. The air crew has hopefully crawled through the foliage and joined our troops adding their flimsy survival weapons to the fight.

A flight of three gunships overhead fires rockets and grenades into the enemy fire. As they pass over the fighting their crew chiefs and door gunners add ribbons of orange tracers to the colorful barrage. The flight of nine empty troop-carrying Hueys waiting to pull the infantry out stand by, circling at 1500 feet a half mile away. When I was younger, I witnessed a terrifying car crash with horrible fatalities. That horrid, grizzly visual was seared into my memory then.

Just now it's being replaced by the incredible carnage below me. You think, "This is hopeless."

Then someone in the circling troop carriers apparently just couldn't stand it any longer. A single Huey breaks out of the formation and dives directly into the enemy fire to try and save the guys on the ground. Based on growing up in Southern California with hamburgers and fries on every street corner, beautiful girls everywhere, the ocean, mountains and deserts to play in, your first thought is a very troubled, "they didn't have to do that."

Then, the very next moment it hits you stark and cold. Yes, they did.

Your judgments can no longer be based on your first twenty years of life. Your new life starts right now, today. It starts over now with the realization that this is what we will do here for others. Most of whom you may never know. But you will take incredible risks for them.

I know what you are about to read will sound like braggadocio, a tall tale. Fiction.

Introduction

I wish it was fiction. In order to do the jobs we had to do and fly the missions we had to we couldn't be nice, wholesome American kids anymore. We had to change. We had to become something else. In effect we had to become monsters. Not heroes. Monsters, to fill the needs of becoming warriors.

Recognizing the barbarian, savage needs of my new life I at least hoped someday, somehow, I could change back. I often feared, though, I wouldn't. Couldn't.

It's not just because you will eventually become one with this incredible aircraft. You will fly it like the machine is purely an extension of yourself. You won't think about the stick, the pedals or the power. You will only think, "Here's where I want to be," and the aircraft goes there. It's about our unspoken Code.

The Code. We lived by it, flew by it, fought by it. Many died by it. So be it.

The Petroleum, Oil and Lubricant dump is where you took your Huey to refuel and rearm. So I'm sitting one day at a POL dump. My crew chief and door gunner are taking care of the fueling. Crew chief is pumping JP-4 into the bird, door gunner standing by with a fire extinguisher. Seat belts off with the doors open as always when refueling to be able to leave in a hurry in case of fire. Ground crews rush out with ammunition to rearm our guns. The helicopter is at idle RPM. It is hot and humid like always. But there is an artificial breeze from the main rotor. My copilot and I take turns getting out of the ship to pee.

You're twenty hoping for more. Healthy. Awash in hormones, horny twenty-four-seven. Sleep doesn't quell that hunger. You figure or at least hope you will survive this war and have another sixty or more years to live. Haven't figured out what to do with that hoped-for upcoming period of your life yet. But you will when it matters.

Maybe be a career in aviation. Yeah. Maybe fly for the airlines surrounded by beautiful stewardesses, making good money with nobody shooting at you. Given the vast amount of time ahead at least you hope you will get, it doesn't appear to be an imminent decision to make anyway.

Introduction

So hot. The heat, humidity and the nine-plus hours you've already flown today make you tired. Guard frequency is always on, overriding all frequencies on every one's radios and reserved only for emergencies. And over Guard you hear a "Mayday." Even hurried, it comes with coordinates or codes.

There are understood and accepted codes in our area of operation like the Parrot's Beak or the Fishhook. Areas nicknamed for their appearance as bends on the map of the border separating Vietnam from Cambodia. Someone's down in the Fishhook.

The Mayday over Guard frequency means somebody's airplane has been shot down and not too far from your position. Or maybe on another tactical radio frequency you hear an infantry unit in a fire fight with wounded. They're calling for Dust-Off. You're so familiar with your own Area of Operation and with constantly monitoring all the tactical radio frequencies all day you know Dust-Off, the call sign for the designated medevac birds, are easily forty minutes away. The wounded could bleed to death in the time it would take for Dust-Off to respond.

It was amazing listening to so much radio communication and frequencies all day that you could isolate on only one if you needed. You had to learn how to do that.

With your entire life in front of you, with all that could mean, hearing that Mayday means it all just goes away. Just disappears. You tell your crew to saddle up and you go. Unless the downed ship is from your own company you likely don't know the crew. And the infantry unit is made up of total strangers too. But still, you go. This is our Code. You go without hesitation because if the situation was reversed, they'd come for you. This is an unquestioned absolute.

You know too that if the disabled bird was shot down, you'll probably take fire going in for the crew. And you'll definitely take fire going in for those infantry wounded. They are already in a firefight. To the Viet Cong and North Vietnam Army regulars, helicopters are a preferred target.

And the enemy knows, too, we will always come for our own.

Introduction

Whatever the mission is you are compelled to act. You have to. The realities of flying these missions, though, is always the same. Going in means taking fire.

But you also know without a doubt if you get shot down another air crew will line up on final and come for you. A gunship team will, without orders, on their own, jump into the fight and create covering fire. More helicopter crews will line up to come for you. And if they get shot down another bird from some other unit will jump unasked into the fray.

And they will keep coming, keep coming and keep coming until everyone's safe … or everyone's dead. This is our unspoken, unwritten yet inviolable code.

As I write this fifty years out of it, it sounds bizarre even to me. Likely sounds to any reader like so much hubris or bravado. Looking back, it seems so unlikely I would have ever bought into the Code or succumbed so easily to the covenant it required. But there is a small, vestigial voice inside that tells me still that as bizarre and foreign as the Code was to the needs of life, of living my life, were I thrown once again into combat, I'd do it again. Instinct. Honor. Something. I don't know.

Actually, I miss it. That bond, that unspoken but unabashed commitment to each other made everything easier in the hardest of times. In times like we find ourselves in now, a commitment to each other like that could solve so many of our problems.

At a time when our nation is divided by self-centered people using the cloak of democracy to veil their motivations guised as political mandates, we need each other more than ever.

But now we stand apart, divided by lies and baseless conspiracy theories. These are as corrosive forces as ever our republic has withstood. Our enemies abroad and the autocracies of the world cheer the liars and instigators on. They laud their wicked stupid efforts and rejoice in the erosion and decay they see in our republic. Replete with the accolades of our known enemies, the liars and spreaders of untruths seek new ways to undermine our rights and worse. They erode our fundamental belief in our own system of democracy, our

Introduction

beautiful republic. And all the while social media spreads hate and deceit.

Maybe we need to be attacked once again by outside forces rather than inside divisiveness. On September 11, 2001, we stood together as one. We united as Americans against a clearly defined enemy. Now we have both the right and the left accusing each other of trying to take down and destroy our republic. Not separate ideologies disparate in their thinking but equally working together for "the Greater Good." But rather armed camps within, employing deceit as a weapon. Americans lying to Americans is our new destructive pandemic.

I'm glad I once lived in a more honorable time when Americans stood together. Indeed, stood for shared values and lofty goals. I witnessed then how it should be.

Wish we could somehow get there again as a nation. The only two times in my life I've felt the pure camaraderie of my fellow American citizens was during the war in Vietnam. Purely and only, though, from those there with me.

And the very last time, right after the attack by Osama bin Laden. What a shame.

War is an atrocity in itself. But after 9/11 Americans stood shoulder to shoulder. We were strangers quickly becoming comrades facing a common enemy, unified in the common goal of defending our republic at all costs.

In Vietnam it was us against them. Naively at first, we all thought "them" should have only been our enemy. But mostly over there it felt like us against everyone.

We couldn't fight Washington, D.C. The Army tried to keep the news from us about all the anti-war rioting going on stateside. But letters from home and guys returning from leave between tours kept us in the know. We were losing against the American public. When you went home, families and friends questioned what we were doing here. You could get a discount from airlines for flying with your military uniform on through the States when on leave. Most would rather not take the ridicule and scorn. So we paid full price and flew in our civilian clothes.

Introduction

Hiding from our own country.

But nobody beat us on our missions. Nobody. Washington, the folks at home, the press, nobody. When we were under fire, we were of one mind, one heart, one firm conviction. We took care of each other like family. Day in and day out there was nothing we wouldn't do for the other guys over there. Absolutely nothing.

No risk we wouldn't take for each other.

I remember going in under fire to pick up wounded. And in a weird separate and tiny part of my mind away from the focused urgency of flight decisions thinking, "I might not make it this time. Might get shot down this time." And always the same answer from that same isolated compartment of my mind, "Doesn't matter. They need me, I'm doing this." Not heroic. Pragmatic born of our singular code. That's how we get through the long combat days and short, sweltering nights here.

But no way do you allow any form of affection in that macho, testosterone-thick environment. So, if you can't actually tell a woman you're scared, at least you can choke back a whole lot of unsightly fears and ghastly premonitions by holding her in your arms. It's something intricately psychic or maybe just simple warmth. It doesn't matter. It works. There's nothing quite like it. R and R's and leaves are for stocking up on this warmth and comfort.

But not with these women on stage. They're untouchable.

The effect of these four women on thousands of G.I.s is disturbing. Unsettling. No one looks away even to carry on a conversation with a friend. Some of us, like myself, concentrate on just one girl at a time.

We memorize her.

Every form, color, nuance and texture of her is committed to memory. Heat, thirst, and fear all drop away as we vicariously slake an older, much deeper thirst.

We embrace old hungers. Dreams of hometowns, grassy parks, bare feet, blue jeans, summer nights, drive-in movies, hamburgers and fries, a girl at your side and safety shines on the faces of many.

Introduction

I watched a couple guys sit back down and cry. Aching from their own lost childhood. Tears, a vestigial carry-over from that very recent childhood.

Most of us think deep down we're running out of both luck and time to spend griddle-hot and wretched-scared in a country none of us think we're saving anyway. Being brave is a rite of passage here. But it takes a lot out of you. If it doesn't take your life or limbs, it will still extract a heavy measure of your heart or spirit. Nothing in life matters here more than going home.

Even the slang here for home, "The World," came from the sheer disbelief in what we see every day in this war. Surely, we must be on another planet. You've got to get back home to get back what you lost. If you can do either.

The girls eventually do their skits.

Then Bob Hope is saying that recently men had reached the moon. "Our men. One in particular. The first to set foot...."

How did it happen? It wasn't one at a time, a smattering here and there, then everyone else badgered and guilted into it. No, it was one universal thought, one fluid action. Every soldier vaulted to his feet together, applauding loud and hard.

Shyly it seemed, Neil Armstrong walked out to center stage. There's no whistling; that would be disrespectful. Explosive applause! 110-degree heat. A minute goes by. Mr. Armstrong shuffles self-consciously. A minute and a half times thousands standing in incredible heat, applauding relentlessly. No one looks to his fellow soldiers for approval of this ovation outbreak.

No one back in The World knows better than these soldiers what courage is all about. It's worn in war like a uniform you never take off. It gets rank. Bravery isn't running out under fire to save a wounded buddy. That's adrenaline and anger.

Courage is a constant and slow thing. It's those awesome infantry guys taking one step at a time through dense jungle knowing an unseen wire could trigger a mine and blow their legs off or end their life at any moment. Bravery empowers you over caution and fear during the slow times at war when you do have time to think.

Introduction

And thinking about all the ways you could buy it here could drive you nuts.

Courage is not flying a helicopter into hostile fire to rescue a downed aircrew or wounded infantry from the enemy. Courage is strapping that aircraft on early in the quiet morning, staring for moment at the instrument panel and starting it anyway.

You know a rescue or a medevac under fire will most likely happen that day. Did yesterday. Still, you go. Every morning you just start your ship and fly off.

It takes a certain amount of derring-do just to get through the day here knowing that the cool bottle of Coke served by the smiling Vietnamese kid could have ground glass in it. Or the apparently unopened C-ration can is booby-trapped with a tightly-wound band razor.

Courage isn't "going over the top" to assault the enemy lines. There aren't any lines and there isn't a top. The bad guys might even be your own Vietnamese "Kit Carson" scout.

There truly are no safe areas after dark. No safe places for your body or your heart for a solid year.

It takes guts just to shut your eyes at night. It takes balls just to be in this country.

But it took a brass set to be the first man on the moon.

That's what this ovation is about. Three or four minutes of standing ovation in 110-degree heat. An instant icon for thousands of brave young men. The just-now uncomfortable hero tries very hard to hide behind a skinny mike stand. He's not sure he should wave anymore. He looks to Bob Hope for direction. Hope is equally stunned by this outburst.

Thousands of us needed to openly salute this man, this warrior. We needed to recognize and applaud his courage far more than we needed to laugh. We're the brave young men during the fear, anger, pain, and noise of battle.

But Neil Armstrong, in the silence of space, in the quiet, unpretentious yet absolute confidence in his own skill as a pilot, taught every one of us here what it truly means to be a hero. Neil Armstrong: a hero for thousands of heroes.

Introduction

NEIL A. ARMSTRONG
P.O. BOX 436
LEBANON, OH 45036

May 24, 2001

Mr. Richard Jellerson
P. O. Box 389
Seal Beach, CA 90740

Dear Mr. Jellerson:

Thank you for your letter and essay relating to our intersection in Viet Nam.

You were among the many who were putting yourselves in harm's way at the time. I could appreciate it more than most, having done the same 2 decades earlier. I just wanted to thank you and testify that there would be a life awaiting you.

All the best.

Sincerely,

Neil A. Armstrong

NAA:vw

Neil Armstrong read an early draft of the introduction (author's collection).

The offered brotherhood gets you through the fighting. The healing you do on your own.

Left Vietnam after two tours flying Army helicopters.

First tour was flying infantry into combat with our helicopters in tight formations. Fly into a hot landing zone and drop off those amazing infantry guys under fire. Go back in as a single ship medevac to pick up their wounded, maimed and dead. Then go back into the LZ with the full flight, pick them all up and fly them off to

Introduction

another small patch of hell.

Second tour, with the serendipity of military decisions, I was Aircraft Commander on General Creighton Abram's Huey. As pilot for the Four Star in charge of all forces in Vietnam it was a real education for a twenty-year-old to see both sides of how this war was being fought.

Discouraging. Depressing. Seemed redundant and purposeless. Felt nothing was gained.

And everything lost ... my youth, the war, perspective....

Graduation, Pasadena High School, 1965 (author's collection).

The planned obsolescence of our lives is old age. Death is our enemy. Like many of us, I suspect, I've looked our enemy in the eye a couple of times. A serious dirt bike accident in the California desert. Vietnam. Cancer from Agent Orange more recently.

Acceptance removes fear. Gradually, or even easily and quickly sometimes, the idea of our individualized conception of our own death becomes less an abstract. Then, oddly, even less a distraction. It's simply a piece of the puzzle, a part of the equation. The inevitable norm.

Acceptance, however, does not explain sacrifice.

How does any human move his life paradigm to a position of sacrifice? How does a person make and accept that decision willfully against the very imperative of his own prescient being?

Like so many other Americans I watched the war taking place every night on television news. I had a friend one year older than

Introduction

me join the Marines right after graduating from high school. He would be wounded at the siege of Khe Sanh. We heard about many of the seniors graduating from Pasadena High School being sent to Vietnam.

And even if I had never met them there was a pervasive sense of doom when news came out that they had been killed over there.

The war loomed on my personal horizon as an inevitability.

Army Flight School

Army flight school was at once a challenge and a joy. Actually, a realization of a lifetime belief.

When I was a boy, my friends would collect baseball and football cards. I didn't. I collected airplane cards. Might still have them in a box somewhere. As a kid I never said, "When I grow up, I'm going to be a pilot!" Never made that claim about being a writer either. Can't explain it but even as a child I knew I was going to be both a pilot and a writer. Didn't have any idea how they each were to happen but never doubted either outcome.

I got my chance to be a pilot by being almost drafted. Almost. Some—well, okay, parents and teachers mostly—said I was having way too much fun in college. Girls and dirt bikes were getting in the way of higher education. So, the grades dropped, and I dropped out.

I had a friend in Hawaii who had a two-bedroom apartment and needed a roommate. So, I left Pasadena, California, for the islands. Found a great job as a checker in a Honolulu Safeway store. Life was good. Perfect job for a nineteen-year-old boy. Surf would go down around four in the afternoon. So, I went to work. Worked until nine o clock when the night life opened up. Nice. Surfing, skin-diving and tall young women vacationing from the Midwest every week. Paradise.

Then one day I got a call from my brother, Greg. So important a call I was paged over the store's intercom to go to the manager's office. Greg told me I had received my draft notice. Well, nuts!

Hawaii, waiting for the next set (photo by Dale Bailey, author's collection).

Apparently, I forgot to let the Los Angeles draft board know that I had since moved to Hawaii. I wrote to them and told them I had moved to Hawaii so ... what do we do now? They assigned me to the Hawaii draft board which had a two draftee per month quota. This quota, filled for eight months into the future, gave me time to find which branch of the military would teach me to fly.

The only branch taking someone with only two years of college was the Army. I signed a contract that said yes, I had been accepted in Army flight school. But if I were to wash out of flight training, the Army would have the right to tell me what my new job would be.

Army Flight School

I passed the physical fitness test easily; I'm sure surfing helped enormously there.

My eyesight was excellent. Reflexes and hand-eye coordination all passed easily. Then came what they called the psychological phase. Seemed lame to me. A board of five officers questioned me with some bizarre queries. One was, "Do you like girls in short skirts?" "Well, let me think. Yes sir, and the shorter the better."

I learned too that Army aviation had a plan, actually a really good one. If you did wash out of flight school, as over half of all who entered the program did, you would then train as a crew chief or door gunner. Genius, really, as you already understood the helicopter and its role in combat. Later, too, in-country, many pilots finished training the crew members to fly, in case both pilots were wounded and unable to return to base.

Later in basic training I learned that the Marines had lowered their college degree requirement to just two years. Could have been flying jets. Again, nuts!

The first time I got into an Army trainer was in an OH-13 Bell helicopter. That's the one with a plexiglass fishbowl bubble up front and what looks like a horizontal oil well derrick for a tail boom. My first instructor told me he had tail numbers from some of the Bell trainers we were using in his logbook from the Korean War. The instructor made some radio calls getting clearances and we lifted off.

Ten minutes into the flight the instructor says, "Take it. You have the controls."

I'm not mechanically inclined at all. But I've never met a machine that didn't tell me what it needed. So, I took the controls, and nothing changed. We were straight and level at a couple thousand feet. Finally, he asked me how much time I had.

At first, I didn't even know that the expression was referring to my accumulation of flight time. It occurred to me to say, "About ten minutes sir." I didn't. But for some inexplicable reason the very first time I was on the controls of an aircraft I felt like I had always been flying, always been a pilot. Still, throughout my life, the most

(From left) Candidates Jellerson and Irby (author's collection).

comfortable place I've ever been is the cockpit of an aircraft. No understanding of that nor any explanation for it.

Some years later in Seattle I was working in an advertising agency. I had a condominium right on Lake Washington and an empty thirty-foot slip. I got a call from a guy with a thirty-foot boat and no slip. His beautiful sloop-rigged Columbia sailboat was called "Tequila Sunrise." He was in sales and worked weekends. In advertising I was Monday to Friday. So, he asked instead of renting my slip how about, would it be fair if I were able to just use the boat on the weekends? A handshake settled the matter. Didn't even ask me if I knew how to sail. Likely would have been a deal breaker if he had, as I had never sailed before.

First Saturday morning that beautiful little boat was in my slip, I went down to the dock with a cup of coffee and studied it. And again, the machine told me what it needed. Might have cheated and had a leg up a bit this time though having read Joseph Conrad, Patrick O'Brian, Herman Melville and others. These authors often wrote about adventures at sea in the old sailing ships. Not sure what I possibly could have learned about sailing modern sloops from them. But something must have sunk in because as soon as I was underway, I felt right at home.

Also, my family roots are in Newfoundland. This huge island has an economy based on aquaculture. So maybe my level of comfort in the sailboat was generational or race memory. My grandfather, Ralph Young, built lobster boats there, three per year from scratch. And last I heard some are still working boats. But whatever it was, I was sailing. I would eventually sail all over Puget Sound, the Pacific and horizons afar.

Still studying the boat, after a bit I raised the main sail and backed slowly out of the slip. Then raised the jib, grabbed the tiller and I was sailing. Saw immediately a connection between sailing and flying.

Lift on an airplane comes from the low-pressure area on the wings top side. This is created by the wings' asymmetrical design whereby the underside of the wing is flat, and the top side is curved. This allows air beneath the wing to move faster than the wind above the wing, creating lift. There you have it, aerodynamics 101.

The only time I heard how well I was doing in flight school was one morning in front of the commander of the flight school in his office standing at attention. I was standing there bracing for charges of being AWOL. Absent Without Leave is a serious offence in the military. But with living in Hawaii for almost a year and basic training at Fort Polk, Louisiana, and Army Primary Flight School I had been away from family and home for nearly two years. At the time primary training was based at Fort Wolters in Mineral Wells, Texas. Later all training would be done at Fort Rucker, Alabama.

My War with Vietnam

One of my younger brothers was in a singing group and would, on a Saturday night coming up soon, be performing in Oklahoma City. Then the next day, Sunday night, their concert would be in Dallas. I had asked for leave to see him in Oklahoma and was told no, you can't go to Oklahoma. I was, though, given a pass for the Dallas performance.

Not to be denied, I snuck off the base Saturday, drove to Dallas Fort Worth and took a commercial flight to Oklahoma to see him there. Coming back to Fort Wolters you didn't need a pass to get on base, just your military ID.

Unfortunately, I got back after 10 p.m. and ran right into the Tactical Officer charged with bed check. And he wasn't happy as his head count hadn't tallied. So, I was put on report to appear Monday morning in the CO's office. They didn't, however, withdraw my pass for the Dallas show. So, Sunday afternoon I drove to Dallas. After returning too late from the concert again, I ran directly into the same Tac Officer doing bed check.

Monday morning early, I'm in the CO's office standing at rigid, uncomfortable attention. The Tac Officer sites my violations and recommended penalties per the Uniform Code of Military Justice. The Major isn't looking at me or the officer, he's reading some records.

Finally, he looks at me and says, "Candidate Jellerson...." We were not yet pilots or Warrant Officers just candidates for those exalted titles. "Your flight record and instructor notes here shows you are nearly the top of your class. As egregious as going AWOL is we really need good pilots in Vietnam. And, make no mistake, upon graduation you will be going there. So, rather than have you drawn and quartered or face a firing squad, for now you are absolutely restricted to this base until you leave for advanced training at Fort Rucker. Is that clear, Candidate?"

"Yes sir, it's clear." Nice to hear I was near the top of the class though.

I began to feel that maybe I was pretty good when we entered instrument flying. I loved it. To my mind it was akin to playing chess. Strategic thinking is required, and you must always be a few moves ahead in your planning. Every time we needed a weather ship I was selected to go with one of the instructors. The weather ship was a single aircraft tasked to go aloft on a foggy or rainy day to decide if the school would see flyable conditions that day.

I would be "under the hood," wearing a device that would not let me see outside the aircraft. All I could see was the instrument panel and I had to totally trust those instruments. Despite what your inner ear or your senses told you about possibly turning, banking or losing altitude, you must absolutely trust the instruments.

On one of the weather ship flights the instructor proved to me that trusting the instruments could be a life saver. He called the tower for a Ground Controlled Approach. GCA's are unique to the military. It requires a controller in the tower with both horizontal and vertical radar readings. In other words, they can see your precise flightpath, airspeed and altitude.

The GCA begins with this message from the controller: "Do not acknowledge further instructions from the tower."

Then it went something like this: "Okay, sir, give me two degrees left pedal, descend at five hundred feet per minute and slow up to forty knots. You're doing fine. Now a little more left pedal. You're almost to a three-foot hover so stop … now. Good. Now do a 90-degree left pedal turn, and on that heading proceed at 3 to 5 knots. You're almost home. Stop now, turn 90-degrees to your right and put the aircraft down, slowly."

Without seeing the ground or anything else but the instruments, listening carefully and trusting, the bird came to a soft, gentle contact with the helipad. The radar installations were only at the approach end of the airfield. So, pretty sure the last leg taxiing back to the helipad had to be handled by the air traffic controller physically looking out the tower windows rather than his radar screens.

At the end of my instrument school phase, three or four instructors brought me into the commander's office one day. Their goal was to ask him in front of me to allow me to go to the FAA office and get my instrument ticket. One instructor said he would even do extra time to get me ready. But the gruff commander said no, there weren't many, well truthfully hardly any, instrument navigation aids in Vietnam.

I would later learn how right he was.

Check rides are fun. I like them. I learned early in Advanced Flight Training at Fort Rucker in the Huey what they were really about. You're pre-flighting your assigned aircraft and the check pilot walks up. He's a stranger, not your regular instructor. He'd ask, "Candidate, are you ready to show me high-speed, low-level autorotations today?"

Your response, "Well, sir, I've been studying and practicing of course and I'm pretty sure.... I mean yes, ... I think I have it." You haven't even planted your ass in the airplane, and you just flunked your check ride.

The response they looked for was aggressive confidence, even cockiness. A better response would be, "Well, sir, why don't you find a seat up front, and I'll show you what this thing can really do." You still haven't put your butt in the cockpit. And you just passed your check ride.

Training and practicing emergency procedures is about flying the machine in exaggerated operational envelopes. The first time an instructor tells you that if the engine ever quits in a helicopter just keep flying it. Gravity and the weight of the machine will keep the main rotor turning like holding a toy pinwheel outside a moving car. And you think to yourself, "Oh, sure it will."

So, they take you out to the field get you in a trainer take the bird up a couple thousand feet and prove it to you. Chop the throttle, drop the collective flattening the pitch of the main rotor, and float back down to planet earth. At three to four feet, pull the pitch and set it down softly.

There are many emergency procedures to learn. There were two variants of emergencies. Land now and do it quickly or land later. Engine failure is one where you land now. And as fate would have it loss of power means you have no choice anyway. Find an opening the size of at least a basketball court and fly the bird down to it. You are still in control. Fly the bird all the way to the ground.

Army Flight School

The great stunt pilot Bob Hoover once said (and I paraphrase), "In a crash, fly the airplane all the way through the crash." The great thing about helicopters is engine out doesn't mean you have to crash at all. Just land the ship.

In a Huey there are precautionary emergencies. One of the land later type for instance, was generator failure. Happened to me once flying an infantry squad out to the boonies. All of a sudden, a big hairy arm appeared between my copilot and me. The big hairy hand at the end of the hairy arm was pointing at the bright yellow light on my instrument panel. Even though he had no intercom he bellowed so loudly over the constant thumping noise of the rotors and turbine I heard him clearly.

I don't know if he had pilot training or was hoping to someday, but he yelled something like, "My God, look at that! Something's wrong!" I saw the light, reached to the overhead and hit the switch taking us to the standby generator. Told my crew chief calmly, "Chief, we just went to standby generator." His calm reply, "Right sir. I'll get it tonight."

Seeing the chip detector light come on is a precautionary landing. The chip detector light is magnetic and alerts pilots when metal particles, chips or filings pass by the switches in the drivetrain. The light comes on when enough particles have gathered on one of the switches. The chip detector indicates that something may be about to go wrong such as an impending gear box failure or engine bearing failure.

In Vietnam though, we didn't want to land just anywhere. Put it down in a clearing and have the crew chief try to figure it out? No. Who knows who is down there waiting for someone to make a dumb mistake like that? So, the chip detector light coming on means get to the nearest base, even small fire support base or airfield where you can land in a secure area.

There were other emergencies that had no assigned procedure. These were considered catastrophic and usually fatal. These might be something such as a transmission freeze or loss of a rotor blade. If there were a procedure for these it might well begin with, "Bend over, grab your ankles and...." Well, you know how that goes.

My War with Vietnam

Then there was this attention getting morbid dynamic to understand called the "Dead Man's Curve." It was a chart illustrating which combinations of altitude and airspeed would not allow for a successful autorotation landing in the event of an engine failure. Creepy to think about, yet we would occasionally find ourselves unavoidably performing maneuvers within that dead man's curve.

Sometimes we could be hovering over a hundred-foot-high jungle dropping supplies to a recon unit. Or hovering at forty feet or so picking up a sling load. With no forward airspeed we would have to go straight down with an engine failure and just hope for the best.

We learned about hydraulics out, engine out and tail rotor out. In other words, these vital parts of the helicopter important to keep it flying have failed. And the Army does not want you to bend their expensive helicopter.

In flight school my logbook showed just under two hundred autorotations to the ground. Civilian trained pilots don't usually get to go all the way to the ground. Most nonmilitary flight schools will have the instructor roll throttle back up from idle to full RPM before they touch down. A hard landing in a helicopter can "spread the skids." This is highly frowned upon in military circles.

Tail rotor out means it has failed, of course. But if you have enough air speed, you can and indeed must now fly the aircraft like an airplane. Enough forward speed will keep the ship somewhat in trim. The problem now though is you have to land it like an airplane as well. Basically, this means coming in for a landing at speed in a ten-degree angle or less to a paved or dirt strip just like a fixed wing airplane.

The trick is keeping the nose straight going down the runway after slowing and touching down. Usually this would be accomplished with the pedals and the tail rotor you just lost. The function of the tail rotor is anti-torque. Without a functioning tail rotor, in a hovering aircraft the fuselage would simply rotate in the opposite direction of the main blades.

So, after touching down on the airstrip the only way to keep the machine pointed in the right direction is the throttle. As you scrub off speed you will use torque again by small adjustments either increasing or decreasing power.

One of the autorotations we trained for was tail rotor loss at a three-foot hover.

You are so low all you can do is "chop the throttle" as they say. This diminishes the torque issue. But this time you can't drop the collective. No time for that. As the ship is already so close to the ground pull pitch on the collective. This increases the angle or bite of the main blades slowing the bird's dropping down and, if you do it right, a soft landing.

Doing it right is really the only option because as in a real engine-out autorotation, you only get one shot at it. Gotta get it right the first time. A hovering autorotation is the only one you do without dropping the collective to flatten the blades.

The easiest autorotations are those at altitude. Army flight instructors would, without telling you in advance, just chop the throttle on you. You had better have been planning on it. Instructors are pounding it into your head: always be thinking, "Where would I go right now if I lost my engine?"

A kind of scary but really fun emergency procedure is called the "high-speed, low-level autorotation." You're only three to four feet off the ground at over a hundred miles an hour and all of a sudden, your engine quits. You have to do a "quick stop" and gain a little altitude. The quick stop is where you pull back on the cyclic suddenly in order to slow the plane down as fast as possible. The nose comes up sharply and the main rotor system acts then almost like a brake. You need to drop the collective, again flattening the pitch and either climb a little or flip the bird on its side to avoid having the tail boom hit the ground.

The flipping the aircraft on its side option wasn't taught at Fort Rucker in Advanced Flight Training. It wasn't called such but flying in Vietnam could have been titled "Even Incredibly More Advanced Flight Training." That's where we learned flipping the aircraft sideways to avoid hitting the tail boom or tail rotor.

Once the plane is straightened out you leave the collective down reducing pitch and as you get close to the ground pull pitch again. This puts the energy stored in the rotor system to work for a soft landing.

Hydraulics out is just an exercise in muscle and manpower. After a while flying without hydraulic assist, you feel like you just did a couple of hours in the gym. The Huey is a fairly large and heavy machine. Without hydraulic assist all controls become incredibly difficult to work. And again, the plane must be landed like a fixed wing. Without hydraulics the sensitive, minute adjustments to the cyclic, collective, power and pedals required to hover the Huey are impossible.

All that said we would learn in combat that the Huey is an amazing machine that almost never has an emergency problem. That 1,100 to 1,300 horsepower Lycoming doesn't stop for anything less than a direct hit in the right place.

And Hueys often brought their crews home riddled with bullet holes everywhere. One at the 116th came back with so many holes it was Red X'd. Army aviation speak for never to fly again. But it became a much beloved Hangar Queen as a cache of spare parts.

Then there was this thing they told you about called "Retreating Blade Stall." Simply put, the tips of a Huey main rotor could be moving at around 500 miles per hour. American helicopters rotate counterclockwise. I mention that here only because I always found it interesting the European helicopter main rotors I flew later rotate clockwise. It may be that as several European countries also drive on the wrong side of the road, they are just being contrary.

The first time I flew a French helicopter I almost psyched myself out thinking, "How will this work? It's all going to be backwards." No. Again, with any aircraft, you don't think about what the controls do. You only think about what you want the aircraft to do.

There is for every aircraft a published Velocity Never Exceed. This is the top allowed speed of an aircraft for structural and safety concerns. Picture a main rotor on a Huey operating at full rpm and the ship is at a speed of 100 miles an hour just to keep it simple. The rotor blades are pitched up because of your speed. The angle is greater as they need to take a bigger bite out of the air.

Army Flight School

The combined speed of the tip then approaches 600 miles an hour going forward. As the blade travels from right to left at the point where it is directly on your nose it now begins to travel backward or retreating. That's where the trouble lies. It's still doing 500 miles an hour but now your forward speed of 100 acts on the blades going backwards. That's a 200 miles an hour difference. And with no new air to bite through it is in danger of no longer offering lift and can stall. The rotor head itself makes an adjustment but there can still be a catastrophe.

They never showed us retreating blade stall in flight school as it was too dangerous. So, they just taught us about it, what to look for and how to avoid it.

But it happened to me once when I had just begun flying the smoke ship. One day my timing was off somehow. I was behind the inbound flight of nine with troops on board. In trying to catch up I put the aircraft in a dive at full speed. Soon the cyclic was sending a strange message to me. It was shaking. In effect, the preliminary indicator of a stall in any aircraft. Slowed up and it went away. Scary though.

Before I went to Vietnam I was really just a happy Southern Californian kid who liked girls, hamburgers, sand-lot football and the beach. The next clear memory I have is that of being shot at while piloting a large, sparsely armed helicopter into a firefight to pick up wounded American soldiers. I was barely twenty years old.

The philosopher who said "Be careful what you wish for" got it right.

It had all happened so fast. Flight school had been a year of intense education, pressure and thrills. Great flight instructors taught me in the forests of Alabama how to knock a specific pinecone out of a tree with the tip of my main rotor blade while hovering a big helicopter in a really small clearing.

More off-syllabus lessons in low-level flying at 100 miles an hour with my skids in the tree tops built confidence. "You can't just pull back on the cyclic stick to climb," the instructor told me. "If you don't add power as well you will drag your tail rotor through the trees." Army flight school prepared me well. Most Fort Rucker flight instructors had only recently returned from a Vietnam tour in combat. They assured me I'd do fine.

Learning to fly was incredibly easy and came naturally to me. No explanation, it just did. Becoming an officer was not as easy, not nearly as natural.

During the Army's intense Primary Flight School, I was busted one morning during one of our regular rigid inspections for having a dirty razor. Couldn't have been that dirty really as I was barely even shaving.

But ... on restriction I was ordered to report to the Company Commander every morning at 5:30 for "razor inspection." Still dark outside, I met with the Commanding Officer in his office. I stood at solemn attention with my razor held at Port Arms. After the third or fourth early morning of failing his inspections, I went to the PX and bought a new "hideout" razor.

Next morning I reported to the CO again. He studied the razor for a long time.

I'm scared he'll figure it out and he does.

Finally, he says, "Perfect. Absolutely clean. And actually ... it looks brand new." Now I know the shit is going to hit my personal fan. He looks me right in the eye and says, "Good for you. You're off restriction."

What? Wow. My blank expression drew no explanation. I figured it out later.

Beyond learning to fly and becoming an officer, he wanted me to learn how to act if I was shot down and became a prisoner of war.

Always fight back. Never quit. Beat the system. Find a way. Always find a way.

A final thought about flight school. Fort Rucker, Alabama (now Fort Novocel), is where all of us young men became either pilots, crew chiefs or door gunners. Thus being "reborn as aviators" gave us the right to refer to Fort Rucker lovingly and with great respect as "Mother Rucker."

Vietnam First Tour, Combat Assaults

Sitting in the back of a Huey leaving Tan Son Nhut Air Force Base just outside Saigon for Cu Chi was a twenty-minute life-changing ride. Only minutes north of Saigon but a world away from everything I knew. One narrow dirt road was considered the main highway. We flew over miles and miles of thick jungle with intermittent clearings and rice paddies. I'm being flown to Cu Chi to fly with the 116th, Assault Helicopter Company, the Hornets.

On the way, about a thousand feet below us, we can see a helicopter flight of nine ships on final approach on a combat assault to a clearing. One of the pilots over ship's intercom tells us, "That's the 116th, the Hornets. You can always tell because they all have the top side of only one of their main rotor blades painted white. They also have the biggest nose art in-country. It's a big nasty hornet. The gun team has a red hornet, and the two lift platoon's hornets are either yellow or white."

As I look down from two thousand feet I remember thinking wow, they didn't teach us to fly formations that tight in flight school. Those guys are good! I would soon learn that contrary to what one might think, it's actually logical to fly combat missions in very tight formations.

The outbound fire from the crew chiefs and door gunner's M-60 machine guns is more concentrated, more intense. The gun team has a smaller, tighter herd of "Slicks" to protect. Slicks is a slang expression for the troop-carrying Hueys only slightly armed with two machine guns. And usually, tight formations allow for having all updrafts and downdrafts affect all the birds the same way at the same time. Landing at Cu Chi we walked from the helipad to the 116th compound.

The entire base isn't very big. There are several infantry companies and some admin Quonset huts. One poorly paved street went around the one-time village now replaced with a short runway in the absolute middle of the base. There were several L shaped sandbag revetments protecting the helicopters. The base perimeter was formed by coils and coils of concertina wire surrounding the base with open land defoliated by Agent Orange.

I remember one morning walking out to the flight line seeing a formation of three Air Force C-123 cargo planes directly over Cu Chi flying right through our pattern. And wasn't it odd they were rigged as crop dusters? The spray they laid down had to be Agent Orange.

The jungle was pushed back roughly maybe a quarter to a half mile or so around the base. This measure was taken to avoid having the enemy sneaking in and getting too close. Machine gun emplacements with built up sandbag barriers were everywhere. There were also armored tanks and other mobile, large caliber guns and cannons like howitzers placed along the perimeter.

The fallacy of all that thought put in to protecting the base was that the enemy had tunnels four stories deep all over the area including, they said, underneath the base. I arrived in early January 1969 right after what was called "Little Tet." In an officer's orientation speech my first day at Cu Chi, the officer said it was believed there were still Viet Cong inside the wire.

Bad news started piling up early.

I was to live for the year in a wooden two-man officer's hooch. Room for two bunks and bookshelves, couple of chairs. Small sandbag bunkers were built under the bunks. There were bigger bunkers close by of course. But traveling to them in the dark during a missile attack could be risky.

After I had been at Cu Chi for a while I heard an incoming missile one night. Hearing the whistling inbound getting louder and

Vietnam First Tour, Combat Assaults

louder it's hard to know, should I run for the bunker? Would I be running away from disaster or toward it? Turns out, that night slipping into the bunker under the bed was the right call. My hooch was right next to the mess hall and that missile took the mess hall out, levelling it entirely. Looked like we would be ordering out for a while.

It was likely more of an economic factor than a carefully thought-out psychological ploy. But one rocket or missile a night was pure genius. Usually, you couldn't get back to sleep thinking there might be another. Probably though the one rocket a night dynamic was purely economics driven. The rockets in III Corps, the area with Saigon and Cu Chi in the middle of it had to be walked down or bicycled down all the way from North Vietnam on the Ho Chi Minh trail.

The dedication and courage of our enemy was impressive. We would hate them for being our enemy and killing guys we flew with every day. But nobody doubted their bravery. Most Vietnam veterans I've spoken to have nothing but deep and total respect for our then enemy. Particularly the Viet Cong as guerrilla fighters they basically had little support, often living off the land.

And they fought fiercely for their country. After all, in their minds, we were invaders.

There were more barracks style housing for the enlisted men. Probably four to six men per hooch. We had an old dusty Quonset hut that passed for a sad little officer's club.

I didn't know it yet, but I had met my hooch mate on the flight in. Charlie Danielson was fresh out of flight school as well, so we hit it off right away. I think he was from the Midwest. A nice guy about twenty, blonde, blue-eyed kid. One of his eyes was seemingly not quite level with the other, just a fraction off. He would become my first ever copilot when I became aircraft commander a few days before he did.

And he, like so many others in the 116th, would not make it out of there alive.

As a bastard outfit—military slang for unattached to a larger unit such as a battalion or regiment—the 116th flew anyone and everyone. We did troop insertions, extractions, and medevacs all over III Corps for different groups. One day we would pick up Cambodian mercenaries to take on the enemy forces nearby. These were teenage boys and very old men, too young and too old to be conscripted into the Cambode military. They were barely armed for combat with antique rifles, wearing tee shirts and shorts. They were recruited and paid by our CIA.

Next day we would fly First Cavalry troops as their ships were down for maintenance. That would be the only time their infantry flew with any other unit. This template of the same troops and helicopters always working together would become the norm for combat assaults. This would result eventually with the 160th SOAR, Special Operations Aviation Regiment.

The camp equipment seemed already aged and antique. The loudspeakers for the camp, the wiring, the porta-potties, etc., all looked like leftovers from another war. Another time. Back home in the early seventies I would watch the great TV series about the war in Korea, "MASH." There I recognized the equipment as indeed much like my first trainer, the Korean War era OH-13 helicopter, leftovers from another American war.

I hated hearing the scratchy tape recording of "Taps" blasting out over those crappy loudspeakers every time we lost someone.

You had to prove your mettle in that unit. Very quickly everyone there would be counting on your skill in the air. Inaugural proof was showing you could drink a "Flaming Mimi" in our officers club. Décor struggled gallantly between rattan furniture and Playmates of the Month tacked on the walls.

First night in the unit you were handed a shot glass filled with bad whisky. Then it was set on fire. The longer you held it racked with indecision or fear the hotter it would get. The trick of course was to flip it upside down quickly and drink it. The flame went out as soon as you flipped it upside down, so the only burning came from the cheap whisky itself.

Only a few weeks out of Army flight school I was a copilot on my second or third day flying a combat assault. Army helicopter crews flew troop insertions, extractions and medevacs all day, every day.

Vietnam First Tour, Combat Assaults

The same missions for up to a full year if you made it. Many of us didn't.

At the Army Aviation Museum at Fort Rucker, Alabama, where all of us trained, there are 4,347 names chiseled into a small, elegant, wall. These are the Army aircrew members we lost there; crew-chiefs, door gunners and pilots.

I knew many of those we lost. Three of those names were friends of mine. We flew together. Their names now on a solemn, gold wall. And still at the edge of my consciousness almost daily.

Mike Goeller. Charlie Danielson. Fred Follette.

"C'mon Mister Jellerson, grab your gear! I'm giving you your orientation ride!" This abrupt, bellowed command came from Captain Taylor, second in command of the 116th, "Hornet 5." In Army command structure the commanding officer was designated (unit call sign) "6." In the 116th, the CO would be "Hornet 6."

After two days at the 116th I had yet to fly. Orientation flights are given to familiarize a new pilot with his Area of Operation, our AO. I would season and mature with this combat assault outfit giving orientation flights myself eventually. We would take a Huey and a new guy up to three thousand feet and point out both the friendly and the hostile villages in case you're shot down. And "Oh, by the way, that horizon over there is Cambodia. Try to stay out of it."

I was so new in country I didn't know if Taylor got a call while enroute or if he just had a perverted sense of orientation flights. But it turned out to be my first medevac mission. Dry season about dusk, Taylor flies us into the middle of a dry rice paddy. And we were under fire of course. There wouldn't be wounded to medevac unless a unit was in a fire fight. This was my first epiphany in-country.

We landed in the middle of the dry rice paddy surrounded by American infantry firing madly into the tree lines from behind the paddy dikes. Ribbons of deadly orange tracers laced out lashing violently at every known enemy position. Couldn't actually see the enemy but their locations were easy to identify from their unrelenting muzzle flashes. From the tree line great volumes of Russian and Chinese rounds, green and white tracers streaming back at us in return fire. Colorful.

A Huey pilot sits about five feet up on the controls just behind a large plexiglass wind screen. It was like watching Dante's Inferno in abstract from a picture window. I remember thinking, "What was I thinking signing up for this just to learn to fly?"

A couple of soldiers hurriedly place their wounded comrade in the cargo bay, and we're off headed for the hospital pad at Cu Chi. Apparently, I passed my check ride as the next day I'm a copilot in a flight of nine helicopters on my first combat assault.

Still early, still wondering and questioning my life choices, I'm flying a day or so later with Lieutenant Tubbs as Aircraft Commander. Straight out of flight school I've been indoctrinated about proper radio procedure. It is crisp, to the point and has definite breaks. They are spoken to illustrate the end of conversation and the end of a call. These spoken comments are, "Over" when you've stated your point and "Over and out" when you end your call. Specific and ironclad was my understanding.

We're at around 500 feet on a long final to an LZ up ahead. In the dry season we flew combat with the pilot's and cargo doors removed to reduce a little weight and I think facilitate a quicker egress if shot down. Drafty sure, but the view was awesome. I could often see the enemy below me several hundred feet, straight down the side of the helicopter.

Looking down into the jungle this day we see North Vietnamese regulars in their tan uniforms and pith helmets running through the jungle. Lots of them. They're not shooting at us while on the run as they're trying to get to what appears to be our destination. A helicopter sitting on the ground is a better target.

As both sides know how these assaults work, some trickery came to be. We would fly in tight formations straight at an open spot in the jungle until short final. Then last minute, at a few hundred feet, dogleg off to the right or left at perhaps a 45-degree angle. The guise was so the enemy hopefully would set up in the wrong place.

Tubbs as flight lead reports to the ground commander about the

Vietnam First Tour, Combat Assaults

hordes of enemy below. The infantry ground commander, in proper radio-ese, tersely asks for the approximate numbers of the enemy. Tubbs' casual reply, "Oh, they're all here." My education continues.

The most casual Aircraft Commander I flew with was another Warrant Officer named Kitchens. Still new and trying to get used to my almost vertical learning curve I'm on the controls as we pick up a squad of American infantry under fire. With my peripheral vision I see Kitchens casually watching me. His hands were nowhere near the controls, and I thought they should have been. We're lifting off, heavy with soldiers. At the edge of the LZ is a tree line we need to climb over.

Calm as ever I hear Kitchens say, as if I'm still back in flight school, "You didn't do your hover check." I don't think I replied to this. Concentrating on nursing this struggling Huey over the trees was taking my full attention.

A hover check is done after picking the bird up to a three-foot hover. Usually performed when not under fire. There is a "Go—No Go" gauge on the instrument panel. Hovering, the loaded helicopter can weigh itself and determine if it has enough power to fly. I willed the aircraft over the trees and flew on.

Later that day, still with "Mad Dog" Kitchens, we're landing the flight of nine ships in "trail" (single file) formation on a dirt road inserting troops into a hot area. All the troops on board, the door gunners and crew chiefs are all firing at the enemy on both sides of the flight. All of a sudden, Kitchens grabs one of the small machine guns hanging between our seats. These smaller versions of the M-16 were considered our survival weapons.

As he fires a full clip out the left side of the aircraft the hot brass ejects out of the right side of the gun. These hit the wind screen and deflect in a perfect arch, directly onto my crotch. Likely I'm not going to catch on fire through my Nomex fireproof flight suit. But still, I yelled at him like he was the New Guy, not I.

The other "survival" weapon was our issued Smith and Wesson .38 with the western holster. First day in combat my AC explained the true value of these near useless weapons. Just before fastening our four-point harness after the engine was running, not before in case of a fire, we would shift the holster into position between our legs in front of our young, precious family jewels. The idea of course was to more or less bullet proof our future. That was the theory anyway.

There was a gallows humor that went with the .38 too. The gun was loaded with only one round. In the event you were shot down that round was for you.

I learned combat flying from Taylor, Kitchens, Tubbs and many more talented pilots. They attended the only reunion for the 116th I too ever attended. Seeing those three alive and well put to rest and eased some pain I had carried with the loss of the copilot, crew chief and door gunner friends I lost over there.

When I became an Aircraft Commander in the 116th I got my own Huey. The crew chief and I would fly together changing out copilots and door gunners every day for a while. The first thing I noticed walking up to the ship was a huge screwdriver usually only needed for diesel trucks. So, I asked the chief about it.

He was an old hand at combat assaults having been in the unit for a couple months already. "Well sir, you see sometimes we haul South Vietnamese soldiers. And sometimes they don't leave my helicopter as fast as I'd like. They balk because they're scared or just move too slow for my taste. Since time spent on the ground makes us a great target I whack the slow ones over the head. And conscious or not boot them off the bird. Also sir, it's never happened in this unit yet, but we know some of the South Vietnam troops are communist sympathizers. Other units have had the last Vietnamese soldier off the bird pull a pin on a hand grenade and pitch it into the cargo bay. Won't happen on my ship, sir."

My simple response, "Carry on, Sergeant." I knew I was in good hands.

And his referring to the Huey as his aircraft was absolutely correct. I might fly it, but he keeps it flyable, sometimes working through the night on it. I came out one morning to do my preflight and found him asleep in the cargo bay. He had been working so late he just dropped off to sleep in the bird.

Vietnam First Tour, Combat Assaults

Graduating from flight school meant not only getting your wings as a military pilot but gaining a new and incredibly powerful belief in yourself. This was clearly part of the training. From graduation day and through my "advanced flight school" in Vietnam until now, that confidence in my pilot skills has never waned. I have always believed I could walk up to any aircraft on any airport anywhere in the world and if can figure out how to start it, I can fly it.

There was more gallows humor that we all gravitated to, embraced and enjoyed in combat flying. As aircraft commanders we traded off flying lead. Whoever Flight Lead was that day would announce for instance, full suppression from our M-60s on the right or left depending on where the bad guys were entrenched.

He would then add on short final to a hot landing zone, "Hornets get your CA lock up." The CA lock up or combat assault lock up was a small lever on the right or left side of your seat that would lock your four-point harness in place. The idea was that if you were shot, wounded or dead, you wouldn't slump over the cyclic and crash the aircraft.

There was a 116th pilot, pretty sure from the accent who it was, but without using his call sign, in a blind radio call right after the CA lock up call he would broadcast, "Hornets ... we're all gonna die!"

Eventually we actually wanted and needed to hear that radio call on our tactical frequency on final approach. Completely counterintuitive of course. But it somehow helped us to relax with the voicing of the ominous and very real possibility. If Mike wasn't flying that day someone else would stand in for him. Amazing how that call would have such a positive impact on all of us.

As a slick and Smokey pilot I was attracting attention from other pilots in the unit. One day the lead pilot for the Stingers asked me to fly with the gun team. It was a recognized compliment to be asked. Crazy as it sounds, I passed on it.

But ... after all, we were at war. The way to win a war is obviously to kill the enemy. And I was an active participant in the war. Yet I didn't want to wake up every day there knowing my job was to kill as many people as possible.

A couple of questions began to cross my mind very early on at

My War with Vietnam

Cu Chi as the reality of facing combat began to sink in. One was, can I accept that I might die here for my country? And the alternate question, can I kill another human for my country?

I struggled with the second question. The first was out of my hands. Some enemy soldier certainly could take my life for flying grunts into combat or picking up our wounded.

I trained to be an Army helicopter pilot knowing I would probably be in a wartime situation. But killing anyone had been repugnant to me from my earliest understanding of morality. But if that were true, why didn't I become a conscientious objector? It was an honorable claim for those who did. And I didn't.

What didn't I understand about my own conflicted decision paradigm?

The enemy below this day was a wonder to see. I was still a copilot on my first or second combat assault. They ran at full speed through the jungle in those light brown uniforms and pith helmets carrying all their weapons. These North Vietnamese Army Regulars were fully committed to get to our landing zone ahead of us. They ran through the humid, deep green, overheated jungle with only one thought: shoot down the helicopters.

At one level I understood their goal this day was to kill me. Still, this was the first time I had ever seen them. I hadn't yet seen them shooting at my friends or myself. I had only been taught that they were my enemy. My country's enemy.

Until then I had only intellectually embraced even the concept of "enemy."

Only moments later at a visceral level, with primal understanding and an irrevocable acceptance, they became my enemy.

This life-changing perception came with the muzzle velocity of a bullet. I was close enough to see the dark eyes of the black pajama clad Viet Cong soldier just now popping up from behind a dry rice paddy dike, shooting right at me. Me!

Hate filled his heart. I saw it in his eyes he was that close. Heavy with troops and on short final there were no evasive measures to be taken for my aircraft. He wanted me to die. I wanted to live.

Vietnam First Tour, Combat Assaults

The Pledge of Allegiance, life, liberty and the pursuit of happiness instantly meant nothing. Death was my enemy now.

My door gunner with his heavy machine gun and the infantry on board were all shooting back at the young soldier. A fusillade of heavy, hot lead rounds poured out of the cargo bay. Everyone on board was shooting back at him so that he, rather than I, would die that day.

He actually disappeared under the torrent of our heavy return fire.

I was fine with that. Still am fifty some years later. Them or me. Death is the enemy. I'll never know who they left behind. But I lived through that day. And many more like it. I had been a new pilot in-country, Vietnam in January 1969. By Easter week I was a combat veteran.

That Easter was unlike any I have known before. As I remember Easter Sunday at home, it is an occasion of beauty and serenity, flowers and new clothes, happiness and religious rededication. Easter church services are full of meaning and ceremony. Sure, the choirs of Easter are a little larger than normal as are the congregations. But everyone is welcome on this day, more meaningful to Christians than Christmas.

In Vietnam, however, there is no time for services. There is only the mission.

But Easter's mission is different.

The mission is to airlift South Infantry Company into a multitude of landing zones patch-worked across Central Vietnam. It is a frustrating and exhausting job as the Vietnamese commanders often direct us to the wrong landing zones. This lack of planning and organization quite often puts us into "hot" zones that have not been prepped by artillery. Or anything else.

After one particularly uncomfortable exercise in this "Vietnamization" of the war, we put the troops out into a "cold" sector and are released until further notice. Our gunships stayed behind to protect the infantry troops.

The nine empty slicks head for a village complex known as the Sugar Mill.

My War with Vietnam

We had been to the Sugar Mill many times before. It's a small, quiet village built around a now defunct mill, surrounded by flat plains and streams. The mill itself is built on the river's side of the village, as is the only road to the area. This road, where it is straight, serves as our standby airstrip when working the area.

We land in trail formation, settling to the ground about twenty feet apart. We let the big turbines idle and cool for exactly two minutes, and then shut down. Eight of the other ships follow flight lead at precise two-minute intervals. As "Tail-end Charlie" again, mine is last.

This cooling and shutting down process has the curious effect of going from total noise of engines and rotor blades to total silence by precise degrees. Usually, this transition from combat chaos to comforting quiet is so awesome there is no talking by the aircrew for a minute or so afterward. It is during this respectful silence that I hear children converging on the ships.

I look up and discover what seems to be thirty or forty children milling around the helicopters. There are more kids here than I have ever seen in one place in Vietnam. It's ironic that I should meet so many here on Easter when every other time we'd been to the Sugar Mill I don't remember seeing any.

They were a boisterous but pleasant bunch. They had lean yet soft faces of light brown skin, big dark eyes and blue-black hair speckled with brown dirt and black mud.

Perhaps they didn't realize it was Easter. There wasn't a frilly bonnet or shiny patent leather shoe among them. Instead, their frail limbs were scantily covered with torn and dirty shorts and now and then ragged shirts as well. Up close, they smell faintly of dried fish and cooked rice. They are pitiful. And so lovable.

They are begging for "C-rations" from the weaker-willed men in the flight by saying "Chop Chop G.I.?" And pointing to our emergency supplies strapped under the troop seats. Being an easy mark for this form of extortion, my crew and I give what the ship can spare and enjoy it.

Eventually sharing turns into a game. It became great sport to throw the canned rations across the large mud puddle on one side of the road. Then watch the kids charge through it, racing for the food. There is always something held back for the ones not making it completely across the puddle.

Back in the world, Easter preparations would be underway.

Parents are perhaps praying for Sunday services while taking a few last stitches on a new little dress. Or sweeping the patio in preparation for company. The roast might already be simmering in the oven.

Young girls will be dying to see their girlfriend's new clothes. Their boyfriends thinking along the same lines.

Here at the Sugar Mill, there is a rare, cool breeze blowing. And it's quiet for a change. The land is very green and lush from the heavy rains. There are hundreds of birds in the air, a rarity in this war-torn country.

Or maybe I just hadn't noticed them before.

The children are cavorting all over the ships. But this was a welcome, pleasant sound compared to the usual one of guns, artillery and aircraft. At this moment

Vietnam is a beautiful, serene pastoral. And totally incongruent with the tortured land I had come to know.

All of a sudden, the peace and beauty are gone, shattered irreparably by a scratching, distraught masculine voice blasting out of the radio with our call sign, "Hornets! Crank 'Em up"

In one minute, all the children scatter. All the ships are running. A couple of minutes later we're flying. The noise is back. The little knot of dread and fear festers once again in my stomach. Those few minutes in what must have been a make-believe land are gone.

"Lead, this is 'tail-end. We're up and away!"

"Roger Three-Three," Lead replies with my call sign.

It seems as if I grew up here. As if I have been in this scarred helicopter flying combat missions all my adult life. There's some irony there in that I had been just out of my teens when I arrived. I felt I'd seen and done enough already to justify being retired or dead.

I noticed for the millionth time the bullet hole patches in my windshield. I wonder why they don't give purple hearts to aircraft. I wonder if with all the mangled people they will ever run out of purple. I wonder who picked purple in the first place, and if he had ever been wounded?

I'm tired. Tired from tension and fear. And very, very tired of tension and fear.

That combat tour is really pretty much a blur. We basically did the same missions every day. And the days could be very long with few if any breaks. I remember putting in my logbook over 13 hours flown in one day. Army records show me with over 700 combat hours. It all feels very much like I really flew only one very, very long mission with the 116th.

Some days and some missions do stand out though.

Some things in a war don't make sense. As if war ever makes any sense at all. Thousands, sometimes millions of people get killed or maimed. Families lose loved ones. Massive resources are thrown into the mix. And nobody wins.

The last righteous war America fought was World War II. We had to prevent Hitler and his ambition for the Nazi empire from becoming the new world order. Japan declared war on America December 7, 1941. Hitler declared war on America four days later on December 11. Every war since has been a civil war either fought against an aggressive communist regime overthrowing their neighbors or the fight against terrorism.

Just before I got to the 116th they had flown a mission into Cambodia. We weren't supposed to be there, but intel reported a Viet Cong prisoner of war camp with American prisoners held in tiger cages. These were very small cages made out of bamboo and other local woods. Certainly, a worthy mission flying in to pick up Americans held hostage, maybe even being tortured. Pilots had told me about the severe torture aircrews had suffered particularly from Viet Cong women more than men. My imagination drew some very unpleasant visuals.

As told me in Hornet lore, it was a night mission. The bottom half of the helicopter's navigation lights were painted black so they

Vietnam First Tour, Combat Assaults

could still see each other well enough to fly formations but would be difficult to see from below. The light in the Hell hole under the turbine engine was out as well. Those orders made some kind of sense. But then it got weird.

Pilots and crews were told to take rings off and discard any form of identification. The Army and unit identifications on the Hueys were painted over. All this to disguise the origins of the attacking force, I guess.

But wait I thought, aren't we the only military over here flying American made Bell helicopters? If one of our birds gets shot down, how do we plausibly deny it was American forces violating the border of Cambodia? Don't know if the order for all of that came from our own higher ups or the CIA but was pure folly to my mind.

There were mistakes and poorly thought-out orders and grandstanding as well.

I was flying the smoke ship rigged to spray JP-4 into the turbines' hot exhaust to lay down a billowing cloud of white smoke. This jury-rigged device was created to cover troop insertions or extractions. I would follow Gun One, the lead gunship with gunships two and three behind me. Laying down the smoke on the hot side of the LZ, the smoke could hide the low and slow flight from accurate enemy fire as they were landing or taking off.

Leaving the Hornets' Nest, the nickname given our compound, I climbed to only a few hundred feet. The intense battle the 116th was in was so close to Cu Chi it was already visible. I'm only three to four minutes out and on our tactical push I hear the fight. Our much beloved Captain Taylor had rotated home. His replacement is a medal-hungry new captain, a new Hornet Five.

There are seriously wounded on the ground, several grunts are badly hurt. I hear Hornet Five tell Gunship Lead to cover him, he's going to get the wounded himself. Gun One's response is firm, "Sir, the Command-and-Control ship is to stay at altitude. Smokie is only two to three mikes out. Medevac is his job."

The C and C ship was the newest, nicest bird we had in the 116th. It not only had special radios, the ground pounder's company

My War with Vietnam

commander and radio operator were onboard as well. The entire premise of the C and C ship is to stay aloft hopefully out of range of small arms fire and indeed, control the melee below.

The captain's response to Gun One is equally firm. "Gun One, I'm going in to get our wounded. Are you going to cover me or not?" Gun One's response is, "Stingers, on me. We're covering five." The Hornet theme was applied everywhere. The gun platoon was the Stingers, the maintenance ship was called the Beekeeper, etc.

As I got closer, I watched the entire disaster unfold. Hornet five nosed his ship over and dived down into the LZ. Landing between a couple bomb craters left from an earlier B-52 carpet bombing, he touches down. Sitting there he became the perfect target. And suddenly two rocket propelled grenades arched out of the tree line hitting the captain's helicopter. The two explosions destroyed the machine. Still, not to be left out I guess, another Viet Cong fired one more RPG.

The rockets killed some of the aircrew and infantry staff. The captain however made it out jumping into a bomb crater with, I think it was, the infantry CO. Now I'm the designated medevac ship. My only flimsy consolation is maybe they don't have any more RPGs. "Gun Lead, this is Hornet three-three, Smokie lining up for final." "Roger three-three give us a sec to line up for you and will cover you in and out." "Roger that."

There were no more RPGs that day, just scattered small arms fire. And the Huey could weather a lot of small arms fire. Some of these gallant ships brought the crews home safely and never flew again.

The very next day I had another surprise. Enlisted personnel, commissioned officers and warrant officers all had separate bunking areas. I was in my hooch reading when there was a knock on the side panel of the hooch. We didn't have doors. I look up and there are four or five lieutenants down in warrant officer country to see me.

"Mr. Jellerson, can we talk to you for a bit?" "Sure Lieutenant, come in, what's up?"

I then once again learned something new about the military. The

Vietnam First Tour, Combat Assaults

captain had filled out an after-action report putting himself up for a Distinguished Flying Cross. I couldn't believe it. I said something to the effect, "He violates our company protocol by leaving 2500 feet with the C and C ship, gets several people killed and thinks he should get a medal for it?" The lead lieutenant said, "That's right. And in the same report he put you up for the DFC too."

I knew I wasn't staying in the Army; knew I was going to go back to college and maybe law school. But as a pilot the DFC is special and yeah, I wanted one.

Then came the surprise. The lieutenant said, "Here's how that works. Since you are mentioned in the after-action report you have to sign off on it. If you refuse to sign it, he won't get the DFC... but neither will you." I knew the right thing to do and did it. "I'm not signing that report. Do you want to tell him or should I?"

Technically a warrant officer isn't supposed to have any other duties but flying.

I liked that. Once in a while though you would be "asked" to contribute to the greater good. One night it was suggested that I should function as officer in charge of the base perimeter.

I'm driven out to my post, and there I meet a sergeant. He's a teenager and after the military greetings and salute are done, he gets right to the point. "Sir, I can't fly a helicopter. But I do know what all these machines guns, cannons, and howitzers can do. Do you sir?" "Haven't a clue sergeant." "Then no disrespect but maybe you can find a place to relax and if I need you to sign something I'll come get you sir." "Great idea sergeant."

We both knew who was really in charge that night.

As a new pilot, you are a "Peter Pilot." This is a pejorative term. And as such, you're told to only use the ship's intercom. You are not allowed to broadcast using position number two on the radio in the console between the pilots. Broadcast was off limits to me unless the other pilot was hit.

Before I started flying Smokie as often as I could, I was copilot one day in a tight formation of nine ships. We had come down from 1500 feet and we're on final approach to the LZ. Keeping my hands

My War with Vietnam

loose but close to the controls in case the AC was hit. I look down through my chin bubble.

Couldn't believe what I saw.

Smokie was directly under the flight maybe only a couple hundred feet. He was straight and level and we were coming down on top of him closing the distance between us fast. Both the flight and Smokie were doing the same speed. Didn't ask for permission just flicked my radio to the number two position and in the blind yelled. "Smokie break left. You're coming up under the flight!" Saw the guy flying right seat look up through his eyebrow plexiglass window over his head and look stunned. The ship broke hard left and nobody died from an accident. It's called target fixation. It means the pilot was concentrating so hard on the LZ he had lost his situational awareness.

Never saw cowardice on either side. We did have a new flight school graduate though fly one combat sortie and ask to be assigned to maintenance. He was nicknamed "Wingnut" and never flew outside the Cu Chi pattern his entire tour.

Worth mentioning that even though all our aircraft in the 116th were Hueys they didn't all fly the same. There's a world of difference between how guns and slicks fly. A slick, until we pick up troops somewhere, are fairly light even topped off with fuel, ammunition and a crew of four.

We didn't have Cobras. We had B and C model Hueys. These are Hueys too but noticeably a little smaller. Bell's first Huey was the A model. The A and B models were what we trained on at Rucker. They were underpowered for the mission and Vietnamese climate.

When they took off in the morning the gunships would be at their heaviest. Burning full and expending ordinance during the day they would get lighter of course. Full of fuel and armed to the teeth they usually took off like an airplane. They would rock the ship up on the toes of the skids pull power and slide down the runway.

Pilots would be looking at the horizon and runway right through the main rotor system. Many times too, the crew chief and door gunner would run alongside the ship until it picked up some speed

Vietnam First Tour, Combat Assaults

then jumped on. That sounds strange I know. But the two guys with chicken plates (bullet proof vests) and their helmets probably took 400 pounds off the ship's load.

Don't know if other units did this but at the 116th, we had a code made up on the fly every morning. This was our "Fruit Code." It changed every day. We knew the enemy often had radios with our frequencies so we would make up names for the villages and bases in our area of operation. One day the nearby airfield at the village Phu Bai would be Lemon. Tay Ninh would be Apple, and so on. So, if we were shot down we could use the nickname to put out a Mayday call only we could understand. Our hope was that it would help us locate the downed ship before the bad guys did.

Not all the missions were a blur. One memorable mission I flew stands out. I was an Aircraft Commander in God-like charge of a million-dollar aircraft, as well as the lives of the three other youngsters in my crew. So young. We really should all four of us be back on Colorado Boulevard in Pasadena showing off our cars and stealing each other's girlfriends.

Dawn is the only peaceful time in Vietnam. But at 6 o'clock in the morning it was already melting into the subtle violence of 80-degree heat, 90 percent humidity. After two months in this country, I'm still not used to the early heat and humidity.

I had just finished pre-flighting my helicopter, making sure the battle-scarred Huey was in flying condition, when my copilot approached with the weather forecast. "Overcast, tops at six-thousand feet, heavy rains and thunderstorms predicted. Sounds familiar, doesn't it? Another blustery day right out of Winnie the Pooh."

"Yeah," I replied, "I've heard that same forecast every day since I got here. I'll sure be glad to see what their dry season is like!" Such is the innocence of inexperience.

My crew chief and door gunner had arrived with the two M-60 machine guns, and a pile of smaller survival weapons. The copilot and I were now in our seats going through the pre-flight checklist and preparing to start the ship. My door gunner, Mike Goeller, was

My War with Vietnam

an eighteen-year-old from the middle of America. He was also the best shot of any air crew member in the company.

"Where are we going today, sir?" Mike asked. "We're working the 'Iron Triangle' again."

"Hell!" "Close enough, Mike." I replied. And then, louder, "Clear! Coming hot!" I press the trigger which shoots a flame into the big Lycoming turbine. The engine starts to whine, the gauges respond favorably, and eventually the large heavy blades begin to turn.

At idling rpm, with all instruments "in the green," I took a moment to reflect. The Iron Triangle is an area of Viet Nam between three villages that holds more well-entrenched Viet Cong per square mile than any other single place in the country.

Years of artillery and B-52 strikes have failed to root them out. We always take heavy fire there. Their tunnel system is four stories deep and twenty years old. It's incredible. They have hospitals, munitions, supply storage, mess halls and dormitories—all underground.

We would get on top of our hooch's roof at night when the B-52s would be carpet bombing. They were hitting so close outside our perimeter we could see the concussion shock when the bombs exploded. Nothing could survive that, we thought. Next morning, the flight lifts off and as soon as we cleared the concertina wire perimeter, we would take small arms fire. They were fierce, tough and determined warriors.

There was a base not far away from our own at Phu Bai. Depending on where we were working that day we could drop in to their POL dump for fuel and re-arm. There was, though, a single Viet Cong in a spider hole right under the traffic pattern.

All incoming aircraft were politely asked by the tower to, "Please don't shoot at him if you get fired on." This was not a regular "No Fire Zone" of political folly. The legendary "One Shot Charlie" was such a bad shot with his antique rifle, it was said he couldn't hit water if he fell out of a boat. So, the fear was that if we killed him they might replace him with someone who could actually shoot well.

The weirdness really piled up in this war.

Vietnam First Tour, Combat Assaults

We are "Tail-End Charlie" again today, the last ship in the flight of nine to deposit troops into the flooded rice paddies of South Vietnam. Today, we only have our own gunship cover to precede us into the landing zone. The mission of the gunships will again be to soften up the enemy undoubtedly waiting there.

Lifting off it's a little cooler now at 1500 feet. I can see condensation being forced off the tips of the rotor blades of the other ships in formation like pure white scimitars as the blades slice through the damp air.

Soon we will have to leave the relative safety of this altitude, which is, they tell us, "Out of accurate small arms range from the ground." The troops on board are loaded down with all their combat gear. I don't envy those incredibly brave young men walking around down there in that hot, humid jungle after we drop them off.

There's our landing zone. We begin our approach. Simultaneously my stomach feels warm and my hands tense on the controls. My mind forces my hands to relax because the tenseness makes for poor flying. But I can't stop my palms from sweating. It'll be much worse at the touchdown point where we have to sit for a few seconds like a wallowing elephant and disgorge our troops.

First few missions in Vietnam my stomach would feel as if someone shoved burning steel into it. Sweat rolled into my eyes. My ears would ring from pure unadulterated fear. And that same ominous question, variously phrased, would scream into my head: "What am I doing here? When will this nightmare end?"

And through all of that I came to learn, my mind will function as it never had before. Icy cool, becalmed like the eye of a storm. My reactions and thought processes were heightened to new speeds and capacities.

There is an incomparable exhilaration to it. Fear washes through in waves. Yet deeper down, in some instinctual primal area, calculations and reactions are being doled out at the rate of hundreds per second. The operative thought is "panic will kill you here."

So, you sweat some. You allow the occasional gush of fear to pass. And simply take charge, always take charge! Marshal all you've learned. Trust your instincts, senses, and skills and do what has to be done. You're okay now.

The troops are out. We're not taking any hits.

Let's go! Add power. Lift off. Lunge for altitude. Get clear of danger.

Start breathing again. And get more troops. It's always like that in a hot LZ.

Now on short final I pick out the spot where I will put my aircraft down. As I come closer to touchdown, I can see we are taking fire from the tree line on my right. One enemy machine gun is already zeroed in on my landing spot. I try to slow my descent, pulling hard on the collective pitch control. But with a heavy load of American soldiers, I can't alter my short final approach or slow my progress much at all.

Looking between my feet on the pedals, I can see bullets slapping into the inundated rice paddy now two or three feet from my plexi-glass chin bubble.

The rounds hit so close now, they splash muddy water onto the bubble.

I pull harder on the pitch control, now knowing I'm going to float inevitably into the line of fire. The main rotor blades are coning upward from the strain. I can hear the engine losing rpm from the immense overload. Just as I resigned myself to losing my feet or legs on this ugly morning, the firing stops.

One of our gunships saw my problem and solved it with rockets.

My ship had lost most of its power and we settle not quite to the wet ground, careful not to get the skids stuck in the mud. In under six seconds the troops clear the ship. All are immediately lying prone on the ground, mud and all, staying low until we leave. Why stand tall next to the biggest and best target the enemy prefers to shoot at. Now, with no added weight, we take off easily, rising hurriedly to join up with the formation and the lunge for precious altitude.

We fly back to pick up the next party of troops. "Tail end Charlie" is the last one out of the landing zone, a very vulnerable position. Also, Tail-end is the ship predetermined to break off formation and make any needed medevacs.

Vietnam First Tour, Combat Assaults

This means picking up wounded.

It isn't that I didn't like helping our wounded. I relished that mercy mission more than any other. I just never became calloused enough for the job. I could never steel myself to avoid being painfully torn up emotionally when I picked up a freshly wounded soldier. Or one who had just been unbelievably mutilated by a mine or a booby trap.

It's even worse when the medics run short of morphine. Some of these seventeen, eighteen and nineteen-year-olds, who haven't even really lived yet, just scream themselves into delirium, into unconsciousness. Sometimes all the way into death.

There isn't an aircraft that can get a man in that kind of pain to a hospital fast enough.

Our mission has been the same all week. Today will be no different. Airlift the same infantry company into the same sector of the Michelin rubber plantation known to be festering with Viet Cong. Our heavy rotor blades sever the early morning stillness as we land on the tiny airstrip next to the ugly fire support base.

The base is a roughly circular, well-armed pockmark of dirt surrounded by acres of bare no-man's land in the middle of a great, dense, intensely green jungle. Often this free fire zone around a fire support base was cleared by heavily armed and armored bulldozers. Sometimes it was cleared so to provide a lack of cover for an attacking enemy by the ominous Agent Orange.

Six American troops nimbly dance aboard in graceful, well-practiced steps. They seemingly ignore the sixty-pound packs on their backs and the untold weight of weapons and ammo.

I spot their squad leader, Sgt. Johnson. He is a stocky, brown-haired farm boy of about twenty. He impresses me as the hard-fisted, hard-drinking kind who would just as soon scrap here as Kansas or Texas. My character analysis seems spot-on when I see written on the back of his helmet, a caricature of the Twenty-Third Psalm. "Yea, though I walk through the Valley of the Shadow of Death, I will fear no evil. For I am the meanest, bad ass, son of a bitch in this entire valley!"

My War with Vietnam

    A little bravado never hurt a man as he steps into the evil face of danger.

    The young sergeant gives me the "thumbs up" sign. All are aboard. We're on our way. Much heavier now, we nurse our underpowered ships slovenly into the air, looking I imagine a lot like fat young penguins trying desperately to learn to fly.

    Penguins, you certainly know, can't fly at all. In this heat, with these loads, helicopters barely fly. It ain't pretty but eventually we arrive again at a cooler fifteen hundred feet. I begin to ready my crew and the young infantry squad leader.

    Over the ship's intercom to the crew and loudly over my shoulder to the infantry, "Listen up! We'll be landing in the LZ from north to south. The gun ships will be rolling in hot on the left. Recon tells us the tree line on that side is full of nasties. So, we'll only have the slicks to give us full suppression on the right. Good news is we'll land in trail so all eighteen M-60s will be covering us."

    I can see that the old veteran, Sgt. Johnson, knows that if recon got it wrong, we would only have nine M-60 machine guns to handle the right side of our flight. If we do take heavy fire from the right, and the gun team doesn't pick up the cue fast enough, we're in the really deep shit once again.

    I know the Viet Cong fighters will be on the run from the first load of troops we dropped off. We head directly for the new Landing Zone. There will be another tough reception waiting for us in this LZ. This we expect. The value of helicopter assaults to hopscotch combat troops to trouble spots had been established long ago.

    Both sides know how important the helicopter is to this war. Our area infantry commanders use troop carrying helicopters to herd the enemy like a shepherd uses his sheepdogs. The analogy ends there however, as sheep are rarely heavily armed, brilliant and determined guerrilla fighters.

    We are closing in on the landing zone now. I look back at Sgt. Johnson briefing his troops. They all give him a "thumbs up" sign, assuring him they understand and are ready for anything. Liars!

Vietnam First Tour, Combat Assaults

I lock my Combat Assault shoulder harness and begin our hasty descent.

My cheeks feel hot and red. And I begin to sweat again as I did at first when facing a hot landing zone. Eventually the surrealness of the situation or maybe the acceptance of my own mortality gave me a sense of "Oh, what the hell...."

Then, no more sweats and hot cheeks.

The LZ appears straight ahead, and we begin to drop lower and lower, doing ninety to a hundred knots. We are flying in trail, single file formation. We're only about fifteen feet apart main rotor tip to tail rotor. This is no time for watching gauges! But flying this close allows us to enter and leave the LZ together. These tight formations in the air and in the LZ, also allow the gun team to give us maximum cover fire over a smaller footprint.

In the landing area all nine ships will flare simultaneously, slow their descent and forward airspeed, touch down for four to six seconds, regurgitate the troops, and flee for safety. Sounds simple doesn't it?

There is no better target in the eyes of the V.C. than a stationary helicopter. The veteran soldiers I carry know this too. As we come to an abrupt landing, and a short slide, the troops lunge out of the ship and flatten themselves on the ground. I give it full power and we leap into the relative safety of the sky.

Every ship is off and as soon as I'm in the clear. I call flight lead.

"Lead, this is Hornet three-three, Tail-end Charlie; you are off, flight of nine."

"Roger, three-three," Comes the succinct but noticeably relieved reply.

We are two minutes out of the LZ when I hear the garbled, inevitable radio call. One of the guys we dropped off only a couple minutes ago is already wounded.

I immediately call gunship lead. Out here we have to act as our own air traffic control. Situational awareness can only go so far. Announcing I was leaving the flight of nine helped everyone with the constantly changing picture of combat flying.

"Gun Team Lead, this is Hornet Three-Three breaking left out of formation returning to last landing zone for seriously wounded. Can you cover both sides? I'll shoot the same approach, but I'll land up at the far end of the LZ. They'll pop yellow smoke."

"Gotcha covered Three-Three. Keep your head down." He responds.

I think to myself, "No shit." Going back in alone I know I can make a very fast approach and, if all goes well, an equally fast exit. Milliseconds count.

This time my aircraft will be the only target in the LZ.

I line the ship up with the field and nose it over. I take most of the pitch out of the blades and bleed off rpm to avoid a rotor over speed. We're pushing a hundred and ten knots, dropping like a rock and the ship is shaking violently.

At about half a football field's length from touch down I begin a long, very "hairy" flare, pointing the nose to the sky to "quick stop" the ship. I can see only blue sky through the windshield and have to watch my landing spot out my side and through the plexiglass chin bubble just in front of my feet.

The ship is light and handling well. And I've already logged more hours in combat flying a Huey than I had driving my '57 Chevy around Southern Cal before the war. I am very, very good at this.

Remember, a little bravado can go a long way in the evil face of danger.

We fall to the ground and slide about a foot, hitting our mark precisely. There is the usual green, white and orange rainbow of death from tracers snaking out of the tree line and returning to the enemy. The gunships overhead blast rockets, launch grenades and behind the pilots their crews lace the tree line with their machine guns.

Suddenly, three GI's hop up out of the elephant grass ten feet or so out the right side. They run and stumble toward my aircraft. The two outside grunts have their arms around the middle guy supporting him, carrying him to the ship. Because of the elephant grass, all I can see is their upper bodies.

Vietnam First Tour, Combat Assaults

I'm watching temperature and pressure gauges on my instrument panel while looking at incoming rounds of fire. Head on a swivel darting around, sweeping through the entire scene looking much I'm sure, like a prairie dog getting ready to leave his borough. My hands are still on the controls, we're at full power and light on the skids.

Why I ever looked back I'm not sure. It was my first medevac as an Aircraft Commander.

When I turn to look, I'm sickened and horrified to see the young squad leader, Sgt. Johnson, lying there with both legs gone. A mine had blown one leg off at the knee and the other one almost at his hip. Blood is everywhere. The medic is covered with blood, and it's being blown all over the inside of the ship.

I swear I can taste it.

Sgt. Johnson's hands are clenched into fists, held tight to his sides. I look at the young leader's face. His teeth are clamped so tightly his gums are white.

I'm not sure what registered on my face, but he saw me looking at him.

And, for my benefit, he managed a ghastly, terribly distorted grin.

I wished he hadn't.

Then, he slowly turned his fist closest to me, and gave me … a thumb's up sign.

To this day I wish I had never seen it.

Wished I didn't see it again just now.

I nearly lost it. I tried to grin back reassuringly. Then, I turned away, not wanting him to see how I really felt. I'm sick to my stomach and feel weak in his presence.

Is this courage or insanity? He had to have had courage to go into combat knowing this could happen. But it will take a different kind of courage now, not knowing what a long life without legs will require of him. And at eighteen or nineteen, with immediate surgery, he could have a very long life ahead of him.

My crew chief hollers, "Let's go!," and we're off again. I swear I'll get him to the hospital in time if it's the last thing this airplane and I ever do. I pushed the ship right up to its structural speed limit.

I wonder if despite his pain, his memories are plaguing him. Thanks to morphine, memories in fact could be even more painful to him right now than his wounds.

I wonder if all the times he ever used his legs might be coming back to him. The running times. The walking times. The football and baseball times. A park. A girl. A picnic. The beach. All these thoughts must be crowding and hurting him now.

The beach would be especially painful. A football game in the crisp, warm, white sand, his legs and feet kicking up bucketfuls at a time like small storms as he powers through the line.

He's screaming. I wish he would slip into unconsciousness until we get him to the hospital. He doesn't.

He stays awake, grimly gritting his teeth. It takes us just twelve minutes to cover the twenty-four miles to the field hospital pad. I stayed low-level all the way to avoid wasting time climbing to altitude. I see him wince just a little as they carry him gently into surgery.

A very small concession to an enormous, indescribable pain.

We sit on the hospital pad with the huge turbine at idling rpm for longer than we should. My crew and I sit in the relative quiet and stifling heat. We're all waiting for my decision to fly.

My screams to myself don't violate the silence. At this time in his life, he didn't have that coming! A man this far removed from everything real and meaningful and loved, fighting someone else's goddamned war deserves better than that!

His parents shouldn't even have given birth to him and raised him for eighteen years just to have him thrown away in this stupid, misguided war.

My first day as an Aircraft Commander and I wanted to go somewhere and throw up. Or cry. Or quit. I wanted to escape this land of traumatizing days and constant death. But deep down, I know I'll have to keep at it as long as I can. As long as I believe I'm doing this so "freedom might experience a resurrection in this land."

Vietnam First Tour, Combat Assaults

Or at least, for as long as I can keep convincing myself that's what we are really doing here.

Besides, I'm convinced all militaries, all governments in all wars count on this. For me it's personal now. Very personal. Never again will war be an abstract. I don't need to understand the politics of this war anymore. They shot at me and my friends. They were trying to kill us. I've been baptized by fire and seen my countrymen murdered with no mercy or remorse.

And that answered my second question. After the first encounter with the enemy, I no longer wonder if it's within me to kill. And while I never pulled a trigger on any gun while in Vietnam, I ordered it done every time we flew.

I run the Huey to full power, do a shaky takeoff and climb almost absent-mindedly to optimum altitude. As I approach home base I hear my copilot reporting in for me. He shows promise. "Hornet three-three-alpha to base. Medevac mission accomplished. Status-Available. Switching to Cu Chi tower. Out."

Medevac missions in the future would never be the same. We did many.

In spite of the medevac companies on standby, ready to assist, ready to go in under fire, flying un-armed Hueys with only that big Red Cross as a hoped-for shield.

We were already there. Already in the shit anyway.

But I never, ever looked in the cargo bay again when picking up our wounded. Never again looked back at what was going on or who we were picking up.

Just waited to hear my crew yell, "All clear, Go! Go! Go!"

Never looked back there again.

Camaraderie plays a big part in combat flying. Charlie Danielson and I arrived at Cu Chi, III corps, South Vietnam, on the same day. We shared a hootch and a makeshift sandbag bunker and became friends. When I became Aircraft Commander a few days or so before he did, he became my first copilot. Ever.

Then came a time later, as aircraft commander of his own aircraft, Charlie and I were in a very hot LZ. Our two ships were the last to leave of our flight of nine. Under intense fire we were taking hits. I'll never forget the sound a bullet makes hitting the super thin metal skin of a Huey. A round hit Charlie's transmission while we were loading up South Vietnamese troops.

No getting around it, he had to shut his engine down. The gun team would probably shoot a volley of rockets into the ship once the crew and pax were well away. There were things in that bird, radios, code books, ammunition and more we didn't want the enemy to have.

I know without any question or even the slightest doubt to this very day decades later that Charlie would not have left me sitting there unprotected. I waited for him.

Danielson, his crew and passengers left their disabled plane, raced across the dry rice paddy and clambered aboard my ship. Dangerously over-loaded, we lurched along a good, seemed like a half mile of rice paddies, purposely bouncing from rice paddy dike to the next concrete like dike. We often took our only lift and forward speed from bouncing directly on the middle of the skid before we finally got airborne. That idea wouldn't have worked in the rainy season with soft, muddy dikes.

Finally, up around 1500 feet I remember looking in the cargo bay and seeing nothing but American and Vietnamese faces all squashed together.

But there was Charlie, smiling.

Getting that unbelievably over-grossed airplane off the ground, gunships swooping down on both sides protecting me and encouraging me was my best flying ever. Still.

Charlie bought the drinks that night. Those times and the camaraderie are gone. Charlie is gone too. Killed in a later mission near a mountain call Nui Ba Din.

Going in under fire is a huge chance you take in order to pull the wounded out. There is a real possibility you might get shot down doing it and get wounded or get killed. You certainly don't pause for a moment to do a risk vs reward assessment. You just go. You have to.

There are differences between states of acceptance or a willingness to give up one's life. Yet the mechanisms that enable a human to accept this as a possible, probable or even an absolute, given outcome are inevitability similar.

The resolve of the passengers of Flight 93 on September 11, 2001, could certainly be sustained emotionally for the time it took them to act. They had only minutes in real time to acknowledge and accept they even had an enemy.

Join them in those last few minutes.

Accept, as they must have, that in our safest of transportation over our own sovereign country they must fight to survive or die trying. Only a little time to decide what to do.

The entire scenario took place in under three minutes, 45 seconds.

They all soon agreed that if die they must let it be for reasons of their own choosing. Those passengers had to know that in fighting to take that aircraft back they could likely die. But their valiant struggle might also deny the terrorists their illicit agenda.

The enemy was clearly defined. The passengers' course of action wickedly simple. Deliberately then, with acceptance and complete understanding, they would try to contravene the enemy's purpose.

What terrorists fail to understand is that every hideous act they commit makes us stronger, not weaker. Not cowed. Not defeated. Every subhuman barbarism they perpetrate strengthens our resolve to eliminate them.

While they enjoy a Neanderthal life in caves sucking goat teats and believe in a corrupt interpretation of a peaceful religion, we live pretty well in this country.

When cockroaches or other infestations invade our homes we call exterminators. The exterminators come and kill them all. We kick back in an easy chair, grab a beer, watch a little late-night TV and sleep like babies that night.

Look at the history of the Middle East where most terrorists are spawned and Islamic extremism festers. Centuries back they startled the entire world with their advances in science, math and literature. They showed the world the first libraries, first codified law, astronomy, the very first universities. Look to where that culture has been.

But look now as the shameful degradation of their society and culture continues per a linear, malformed perception of their religion. One wonders where they would be today but for this devastating, counterintuitive perversion of a belief system.

Imagine from their earliest blossoming civilization where they and their science might have taken the rest of the entire world. Their scientists and statesmen might have already created cures for cancer, Alzheimer's, poverty.

Tough reading. I haven't come to the part in the Koran about honor killings, female genital mutilation or women as a subservient subspecies. Stoning or death to apostates who decide another religion might fit them better hasn't appeared yet. I'll keep reading.

They long for a culture outlined by the Koran for a world seven hundred years ago. Sadly, also lost in time, they forget December 7, 1941. Another fierce culture made a life altering catastrophic mistake then too.

Every aggressor who has ever come after America, indeed the West, has lost. Terrorists deserve the same. Come after me like a man with a spine on a named battlefield and I'll meet you there. All of us will.

Cowardly, despicably send a woman who thought she was loved by you with a bomb unknowingly in her carry-on into a commercial airliner like you did with the Pan Am flight over Lockerbie ... justice, poetic or otherwise, will prevail.

Send suicide bombers to our concert halls and coffee shops ... extermination as humanity's parasites is the only appropriate response.

Terrorists won't take this country down. Neither will China, Russia or the isolated despot in North Korea. No, we will as a nation withstand all the perils from outside. Then potentially destroy ourselves from within by the two most insidious of decays and caustic of perils: political correctness and divisiveness.

America is going through a strange metamorphosis. Cops stop me in Switzerland for speeding. I have to show them my driver's license and prove my citizenship with my passport and entry visa. They can rightfully ask me what am I doing there? Am I in their beautiful country legally? They have fought hard and worked hard for centuries to create a free sovereign state with rights, protections and privileges for its citizens. Sound familiar?

In America, these pertinent questions by law enforcement are now shamefully often viewed as civil rights violations or harassment. What's next, time out with their faces in a corner for convicted murderers?

Kill to live. Or kill and die rather than have your life taken from you. An amazing short journey. Tough life decisions are those such as career choice, where you will live? Who will you marry?

Kill or be killed is one of the easiest decisions humans or any life form makes.

Everyone on Flight 93 died that day. For the passengers, the enemy was death.

For the soulless, extremist thugs, their day was going to end that way anyhow. Perfect. But now, if one believes in Hell, they share bunk space with Hitler, Stalin and Pol Pot.

Fighting for one's life at the expense, indeed the sacrifice, of one's own life is well documented.

Historically men have fought through the ages for freedom and liberty, resources, family, land, conjured up borders and esoteric ideals. These wars, initiated by so few, often end in the death of so many. Ultimately, there are always innocents. During the 1850s England's armies were always somewhere fighting what Rudyard Kipling would term "The savage wars of peace." Over a century and a half later these savage wars of peace continue.

The innate will to live, the determination that another won't take one's life away is an egocentric mandate. This imperative worth fighting and killing for exists throughout nature. Animals and plants alike know this fight.

Each of us has an overriding contract implied with our own being: Live.

A terrorist then who sacrifices their life, their twenty something years as a healthy human is an aberration, a biological anomaly. We in the West call them terrorists. They call themselves martyrs. Their selfies are likely captioned "Hero."

History will determine their much lesser, loathsome place as common, despicable murderers, foolishly taken in by a splintered perversion of Islam.

Their parents, if steeped in the same deviant value system, are at once perhaps proud of their suicidal spawn. But certainly, they mourn. There would need be a profound sense of loss regardless of the dogma and hubris. After all, what was the point of sexual congress, childbirth, schooling and parenting to toss it all away in the name of misguided and misled religious fervor?

Perhaps they endure a curious mix, an inseparable morass of feelings combining a sense of both deep loss yet a troubled pride at the sacrifice of their children to a senseless Jihad. Akin perhaps to the American parents who lost children to the war in Vietnam, Iraq and Afghanistan?

Born geographically by chance anywhere but the Middle East a single, young suicide bomber might elsewhere live out a full life. Not listening to a cleric or elder explain, "What the Prophet ... really meant ... when he said...," could have meant a long life on this planet.

Interpretation of anyone's "gospel" according to Jesus, Mohammed or Smack Ramen should always come with the caution, Caveat Emptor. Buyer beware.

Rather, these young Islamic pliables were taught as children to believe in ethereal rewards. "Surreal rewards await you in the hereafter if you sacrifice your eighteen to twenty-something years of life," they were told. "Your death is the purpose of your life and could be of no higher value or importance."

In this perverted vision of Islam these "pig in a poke" rewards are believed due them in the life eternal of myth. Sad, deplorable, ticking clocks of young lives wantonly wasted for a religion, which understood properly, not interpreted by heretics and extremists, believes in and longs for so much more.

The terrorists who hijacked all four flights that day had years to commit to their decision. Birthed and raised in this culture of hate—they never had a chance.

Conversely, the sacrifice by passengers of Flight 93 is at once tragic and noble, an epic heroic odyssey. A triumph of good over evil that would make Homer and Joseph Campbell both proud. And purely logical within its context.

But terrorists are not alone. There's a pattern here. Youth at the apex of their power and with life full in front of them yet sacrificing their lives is not purely a middle-eastern or religious phenomenon.

Nineteen Army Rangers in 1993 died in Mogadishu for a credo; "Never leave anyone behind!" Wounded or dead, you bring them home with you. These young men all died for the body of an Army helicopter pilot trapped in his downed Blackhawk aircraft. He was dead before the young Rangers ever moved toward his hostile position. And likely, they knew it.

September 11, 2001; the other "Day That Will Live in Infamy." If you are old enough you realize that saying; "The good old days" now has a specific before and after date. Along with 2,667 innocents in the towers and 156 innocents on the planes, 317 firemen lost their lives.

The firemen, amazingly, were already prepared to die if they must. As part of their value system, their credo, they were ready to sacrifice their lives to save others.

They did. They were running into both buildings as others were trying to run out.

To truly embrace as your option, not just a catchy slogan or bumper sticker, "Your life is worth more than mine" is an incredibly noble commitment. But not logical. If life is the imperative, willfully giving it up is an anomaly. Baldly, acutely an aberration.

The suicide bombers of September 11 had to sustain their conviction for years.

So do firemen and policemen. They wake up every morning to the fatalistic acceptance that it could happen. They could die that day. Fire is one enemy, deadly criminals another. Both groups train hard to have their people see survival at shift's end. But, if irrevocably demanded, they will sacrifice themselves for the rest of us.

Young Army Rangers and other elite military groups are taught that if you are a chosen member of this special team you proudly accept the credo of sacrifice. Indeed, all military branches work hard to weed out those who can't accept the possibility that they may be asked to die for their brethren.

Actually, they don't "Put it in you." They don't "make you," as the ads suggest, "Army Strong." They find those who have it in them. Then all militaries around the world cultivate and nurture that spirit relentlessly into dedication and monastic conviction.

Looking back now I can't imagine me deliberately flying an aircraft into enemy fire from automatic weapons to pick up wounded soldiers. But in a strange paradox, I can't imagine not going in either. I'm at the mercy of my own being, my own conflicted paradigms. Perhaps we all are.

The drives at the time seem now a complex mix of anger and confidence in my abilities as a pilot pushed to the outer edges of cocky arrogance. And the men around you counted on you. We counted on each other. And someone you've never even met truly needed you just now—this last the most important drive of all.

Scientists have been in awe of the basic imperative of life for centuries. Within the last decades they have discovered life precariously but resolutely surviving in such diverse and hostile environments as Antarctica and the ocean's deepest abyss. Nature's injunction to animals, plants and humans alike is "Live!" Whatever it takes, whatever the cost, live.

Newborn babies understand the imperative of life. They scream and cry their determination, gulping in air instinctively, demanding to live. Yet within twenty to twenty-five years of that first breath, the average age of an Islamic suicide bomber or an Army Ranger, some of these young reverse their commitment to the most basic of human mandates.

We can be taught to deny the imperative our own consciousness demands of us.

Vietnam First Tour, Combat Assaults

Through careful training, discipline and the consecration of a value system extraordinaire, some will willingly, sometimes perhaps eagerly, face death.

There is a process whereby resolutely, people release their will and commit their own life for a cause, for a credo. For a stranger. Sacrifice their life for a belief, an adopted higher calling. In a sacrificial act within a religious belief system, no matter the obvious aberration of same, humans have proven willing to sacrifice themselves. The reasons someone vows to martyr themselves or commit suicide are in direct contravention of human nature. And usually as well in violation of the basic tenants of their very own faith had they studied more assiduously.

How does an individual arrive at a decision diametrically opposed to both imperatives; one our nature, the other religion?

Suicide or murder in the name of anyone's "God" violates the basic ideologies of every major religion. Yet in countries where there is no separation of church and state the cleric is an authority figure. From earliest childhood certain Islamic cults prepare their own children early for a future jihad of hate and murder and self-destruction.

Suicide is the Western name for their act. In their own eyes they are soldiers and martyrs for the holiest of causes. The term jihad means "Holy War." They are taught first to believe in the life hereafter. Then the truly devout are further convinced that killing infidels, their own apostates and other non-believers will mean a rewarding life after death in the highest state of paradise.

Suicide soldiers entered Western awareness briefly in World War II with Japan's Kamikaze pilots. Then barged into the collective consciousness again in the late seventies in Iran with Ayatollah Khomeini. But beginning centuries earlier there has been a geometric evolution of religious suicide bombers.

Perhaps it has not outpaced the commensurate rise in population. Maybe it's only through the constant onslaught of media that it's become more intrusive into our consciousness.

There are mechanisms in the West to allow our own youth to die for a cause. This training, nearly monastic-like asceticism, explains how a young man from a Norman Rockwellian hometown in the Midwest becomes a willing martyr for a creed like that of the Rangers, Navy SEALs, and our Special Forces.

A mission we often flew was prisoner pickup. After a firefight or battle there could often be captured enemy soldiers to interrogate. We would fly in, usually only a single ship once the ground commander gave it all clear.

Often too we would take their wounded and medevac them to one of our field hospitals. Along with the wounded, one of our infantry troops from the recent battle came along as prisoner guard.

There was on this one prisoner pick up mission I flew, a grunt ground handler who was guiding me to land where he wanted me. I was watching him and didn't see all the Viet Cong dead until I touched down.

There were many dead scattered about the LZ battlefield. But the closest one to me was lying face up against a rice paddy dike. He was horribly mutilated. Watching a movie later in life, I think it was "Braveheart," the friend I was with commented about the weapons they fought with being so horribly barbaric.

They could actually cleave each other in half almost with their big broadswords or run each other through with spears. Technology has improved war weaponry exponentially. And, to my mind, the military industrial complex excels at outdoing the old-time barbarism by far.

This young soldier looked like he had been hit with a Flechette rocket. Simply put this small rocket has a proximity fuse. Aimed at infantry troops it is designed to go off above them releasing hundreds and hundreds of nails or darts. The effect is devastating. When it's close enough to a human those many nails will literally strip the flesh off them right down to the bone.

All there was to see and understand about this once human being was his cold lifeless face. And it looked like the face of a teenager. Or maybe a twenty-year-old, like me. In the heat of battle, I couldn't think about it much then, there could still be enemy activity close by. My ship was still at full power, my hands on the controls

Vietnam First Tour, Combat Assaults

just in case. But later I thought about that haunting visual a great deal.

Without the deranged thinking of some nation's leadership that boy I saw might have been a friend of mine. Maybe even a teammate if he had gone to America to study at one of our colleges.

If he was around my age he would have grown up at war every day of his life. The French in 1946 tried to reclaim lands they had lost in Vietnam to the Japanese in World War II. He would be too young to be taught to hate the French invaders. But in 1954 he would be nine or ten. Just coming into his own. And just in time to teach him to hate Americans.

I'm certain that in his whole life he had never seen a supermarket with aisles and shelves filled with fresh food or a lush green city park inviting him for a walk.

Unlike me growing up in America, he had likely never known a day of peace in his life. Indeed, his life had been sacrificed to war long before this day. From birth he would need to be prepared to fight enemy invaders of his homeland. His entire life as a human being had to exist in the total void of humanity that is war.

I'm not the scholar I wished I was but our entry into Vietnam was 1954. And would be incidentally, the second proxy war we would fight against China and Russia. The Korean War would be the first. And even without American boots on the ground there, the latest proxy war with them is currently underway in Ukraine.

Every Christmas and Thanksgiving Americans celebrate the holidays by overeating. At the time I had seen nineteen of both holidays. The young soldier was likely in some dark, dank tunnel on those same days eating rats and rice. And that, so he could stay just barely healthy enough to die fighting for his homeland.

As I was growing numb to the carnage to get through that war it would be a long slow trip around the world before I found my own humanity again.

The natural will to live is firmly hard-wired into our DNA. Yet an ideology or a cause can act like virus-laden software that overrides and undermines this firmly entrenched protocol. How and

My War with Vietnam

why does someone circumvent their own will to live and decide, "My death, my me, is worth less than your life"?

Any organism's life, its survival, is its mandate at all costs. The penultimate imperative.

The enemy is death.

All that is left now are the memories of that first tour. And why should I bother with them? For all the pain and anguish they bring. For all the nights of little to no sleep, troubled if it comes at all. I would do well to forget! But I couldn't forget if I tried.

There will always be Mike Goeller, my Midwest, corn-fed door gunner. Sometimes, alone late at night, unbidden, the memory of him slips in on me, still.

Mike was a farm boy, an excellent marksman, and the best door-gunner I ever had. He also became a very good friend. He was a big, broad-shouldered type; soft-spoken, easy-going, big-hearted and very open. I know for a fact none of his friends ran short of funds on their leaves or R&R's. Yet he never took one himself.

Truly his only serious shortcoming was a knack for getting his sandy colored hair cut as if the barber had placed a bowl on his head and snipped off any hair showing. This always made him look like a big, friendly giant.

Or one of those trolls of Scandinavian folklore. Bigger though.

With a company policy of changing aircrews constantly, how Mike came to be my permanent door gunner is a story in itself. He had flown with me randomly on several occasions. After one particularly hairy mission, he said he would rather fly with me than any pilot in the company.

Actually, what he said was, "I would fly straight into hell with you if we had to cause I know for sure you would fly us back out." I took this to be a pilot's supreme compliment and one I still cherish.

A few days later, I had reason to return this high praise.

We were making a nine-ship troop insertion into a very, very hot LZ. We were the last ship in the flight and providing full suppression on the right—Mike's side as well as mine. Usually, aircraft commanders took the left seat per aviation tradition. I preferred the right seat in helicopters, the left seat when I fly fixed wing. Weird but I also always take my sunglasses off on short, short final with either aircraft. No explanation.

Since we were, again, the last ship that day, I knew Mike would be watching and firing in the right rear quadrant of the aircraft. I had picked my spot to land. The dry rice paddy had a two-foot-high dike about ten feet to the right of my touchdown point. With only a second to go before landing, we were moving slowly forward and settling rapidly to the ground.

In my peripheral vision I saw a figure in black pajamas pop up, chest high over the dike. This had become a common tactic for the VC in the dry season. Common because it was so effective and successful. In that millisecond before touch down, I turned to look at the figure and saw a Viet Cong soldier with an AK-47 automatic rifle pointed at my face. My fear was so complete and intense, my mind completely blanked. I was incapable of even thinking the words, "Mike, cover me!"

But Mike had seen him, calculated range and trajectory, and quickly swung that heavy M-60 machine gun forward and pulled off a quick lethal burst. All that in the time it takes to blink an eye and see your short, precious life pass in review.

That night, I bought a round of drinks in the enlisted men's Quonset hut club.

Mike and I flew together always after that. We talked a great deal at makeshift airfields in the middle of nowhere, shut down after a flight, waiting for the call back to action.

I learned about this big man's love for little children. He managed to find them, and they him, when we stopped near a village. He would always design some fascinating game that the children absolutely loved, right on the spot.

His intense love for kids did get out of hand though. Once he smuggled a small boy into the cubby hole beside his door-gunner's seat. He knew we were going to a cold landing zone and coming right back, so he gave the kid his first and probably, his only helicopter ride. I just happened to look back as he was putting the child down after we landed back at the village. I was angry when I told Mike never to do anything like that again. But my heart was never really into scolding him.

I knew from our conversations that Mike had been drafted and hated the Army. He was just marking time, "playing the game," until he could get out and return to his family and land. He had a wife, only a bride really. They had been married only a couple of weeks before he left for Vietnam.

When Mike heard about his wife's pregnancy he lost all semblance of order.

He stopped total strangers to tell them about it. He bubbled over with happiness like the child he still was himself. He would physically stop an officer, address him with, "Hey, guess what?" And proceed to tell him about the expected arrival.

Only the most hard-nosed, callous, jerk officer in the world would have reprimanded Mike for his breach of military discipline. To my knowledge, none did.

Mike had a plan. A plan born in a dream. When he got home, he would take his wife and baby who would be about three months old by then, to a special place he had on a mountain top near home. He would take a tent and food for a month and just get to know them. No guns. No noise. No people. No helicopters.

Just his wife, his baby and him, loving each other. Mike would be nineteen by then. It was a beautiful dream.

With the baby's due date approaching, Mike tried to get special leave to go home while his wife had their child. He applied at Company level and was refused. So, he went over their heads and applied at Battalion level. Refused again and caught some flak for doing that. He offered to extend his tour of duty when he returned. Nothing. Door-gunners were desperately needed.

Mike gave up. He resigned himself to meeting his child when they were both a little older.

One day, months later, all the 116th troop carrier birds were down for maintenance. Our Stingers, as a heavy gun team was tasked to go out in support of some ground troops working the "Iron

Vietnam First Tour, Combat Assaults

Triangle" again. The gun team was short a door-gunner. Mike was asked to go.

He should have never flown with anyone but me.

The afternoon was dry, hot and windy. The gunships had run into real trouble only two miles from our base at Cu Chi. They were taking very heavy fire from an invisible enemy concealed in the dense foliage. The gunship crew members were wearing the new "bullet-proof helmets." These helmets were designed to withstand up to a .30 caliber bullet. So, the odds against what happened were incredible.

But nevertheless, Mike took a hit, probably in his forehead. Constructed to keep injury at bay, the helmet captured the bullet and held it inside, ricocheting around and around until its energy was spent. There was nothing recognizable left of Mike's head. When the ambulance met them at our air strip I could see Mike's blood splattered all the way up to the gun ship's windscreen.

I was first stunned. Then hurt beyond anything I had ever felt in my life for the loss of this farm boy I had grown to love.

But the pain had only just started.

Two days later a message arrived for Mike through the Red Cross. His wife had given birth to a healthy baby boy. Seven or eight pounds, I think it was. I had filled the interim two days with grieving, drinking, some weeping, and lots of bad flying. This message very nearly shattered what little composure I had left.

I knew that the Red Cross message notifying Mike about his wife and baby would take about two days from the states. The messages had to pass each other in the mail and the two occurrences might have happened within a day of each other.

If not on the very same day.

To describe my feelings then is beyond words. Anger, frustration, pain and remorse are just empty collections of assorted letters. Compared to the abysmal loss I felt, language failed me.

I felt a door shut behind me. The passage I was making from who I was, to who I would become, was clearly one way. There was no going back. Ever.

My War with Vietnam

Flying through Agent Orange on a daily basis in 1969 meant I contracted lymph node cancer in 1995. My family was in medicine but encouraged me to go to the Veteran's Administration. I beat it.

Dr. David Wilbur was the VA head oncologist and over the next twenty years of checkups became a friend. He reminded me once of my reaction to his diagnosis of cancer. "Doctor, you're late, I've already handled this. I'm over it. Do what you have to do." David says, "Well let's schedule you for chemo." "Schedule me hell. I'm here right now, let's get after it."

He asked once after I was declared cancer free if I would talk to other vets about my attitude. Usually happy to help others, but told him I don't know where that attitude came from, it was just me. I didn't conjure it up and didn't know how to pass it forward.

When I go to the VA hospital for checkups though and see a guy my age in a wheelchair with no legs, I wonder. Just in my own quiet, private hell, I wonder if it's one of the guys I picked up over there.

Can't know. Beyond that first medevac I never saw who we were picking up. We were under fire and they needed medical attention as fast as possible. Fly the mission, get them to the hospital pad as fast as you can. You don't check IDs. You just know they are wounded. At the hospital pad they are taken off the airplane by hurried, dedicated medics. You don't really ever know if they had only lost a leg or bled to death on the way.

And I don't want to know now.

After flight school my pilot education began all over again as a newbie. In that unit you had to have around 300 hours in combat and the unanimous vote of all the Aircraft Commanders in your platoon to make AC yourself. I switched to the left seat as AC with 270 hours.

My first mission was a nine-ship combat insertion. As a new Aircraft Commander, you flew "Tail End Charlie" last ship in the flight of nine. This assignment was in case your formation flying wasn't fully developed or fully trusted yet. Tail End was also the designated medevac ship for the obvious ability to break out of formation easily without interrupting the flight.

First day as AC and I get my first medevac. Seared into my

consciousness moment by moment I still fly that mission almost daily. Some grunts are dragging most of what was an American soldier, a kid my age, on board my aircraft. And there's so much blood. It's everywhere. Picked up by rotor turbulence and flung diluted all over the aircraft—it turns pink.

It's on windshields and gauges, flight suits, hands and memories.

It's so ugly, real and scary that the boy who loved burgers and beaches hides under the covers in the back of his mind. Flying in combat, I learned to drink scotch neat so I could sleep. Subconsciously, I soon learned to cauterize my emotional system to avoid being wounded, healed and wounded again.

The carnage and trauma hit you so fast so hard there was no time for scabs to form anyway. I was flying right out of my childhood at 110 knots, four feet over the rice paddies of a country I didn't know in a war I didn't understand.

Nothing I had ever done, learned, read, watched, or believed prepared me for the days ahead or the years to follow. And absolutely nothing prepared me for the lingering daily, crystal clear memories that are still not getting fuzzy around the edges. That year and a half changed me forever.

In some ways I believe I'm better for it. What I learned about myself, human nature, and the value of life has shaped many decisions and attitudes since.

Treat every day since the age of twenty as a gift and it will impact your life. There's a price to be paid for that education, however. I'm still paying tuition.

At times awakening too early or too fast, caught mid-dream for a second or two, I lie in bed grappling with a dream-like reality. "Where am I?" It takes a second or so to separate myself and my immediate surroundings from the warm womb of sleep. In these first few vulnerable seconds I'm always in limbo. Coming from that moment of sleep into reality in Vietnam always resulted in a door slam flash of panic, "What will happen today? What will I do ... or see?"

Panic would then ebb. Logic would take charge and my day

My War with Vietnam

would begin. A mix of logic, instinct, excellent training and fear pervaded my every action while in combat. There is not a more dependable coalition of processes to assure survival. When all are fine-tuned, working in concert, your odds for survival as a pilot in combat are vastly improved.

There are times these powers or senses and a fine aircraft are all that stand between living and dying. The people at the Lycoming Engine and Bell Helicopter companies should be publicly lauded. They built a flying tank. It was amazing how many bullet holes and damage the Huey would take before it ever gave up on its crew.

The air combat assault was developed specifically for the war in Southeast Asia. Now a proven concept it's adapted and evolved to fit nearly any war. Simple concept really, soldiers are airlifted instantly by helicopter to any spot on the map. Mobility, speed, and flexibility are the obvious strategic advantages. For their purposes, the gun ship teams worked very well on combat assaults.

They are morbidly intriguing to watch.

A crack gun team will work together like two rows of teeth. The upper and lower rows combine to grab and hold—chewing, gnawing, tearing and applying constant pressure in the right places to keep their prey from escaping as they work one high, one or two low, covering each other and blasting hell out of the LZ.

The noise of machine gunfire and the smell of cordite on a combat assault are unbelievable. What always amazed me too was how much machine gun fire from both sides never hit anything at all.

The military industrial complex was always trying to find new weapons for us. My second tour flying Abrams he showed up one morning with a prototype of what would become gyro-stabilized binoculars, I think from Sony. They were huge and heavy, but Abe scanned the country below all that day.

Then there was the pilots' emergency strobe light. Small and light, the idea was if you were shot down you could use the strobe to identify your position to the search and rescue folks. Great idea but the first lenses were red. Unfortunately, this meant using the strobe at night to attract the attention of a helicopter coming to your aid could put them right off your rescue. At night, the red lens made your rescue strobe look like a muzzle flash. The next version had blue lenses.

I liked flying Smokey as it wasn't gunships or formation flying. Discovered that in the Army both pilots and paratroopers can refuse to take a mission with impunity. I did it only once.

One morning at the 116th I came out to the smoke ship to find a metal tank installed under the jump seat between the crew chief and door gunner. Going into flight ops they issued gas masks for my crew and me to be worn at all times under our helmets. Some clever civilian back in the world figured as long as I'm going low and slow shielding the flight with smoke why not run hoses from a tank filled with some deadly gas and disperse it behind the ship along with the smoke?

I took the mission and flew right into a hot area not far from Cu Chi. Did a pass, took fire, broke off and told the gun team I was headed back to base. I landed and went to flight ops and told them they needed to find someone even dumber than me to fly that bird. The deadly gas under pressure wasn't the problem, I explained. It's not the gas that would kill us. The real problem was if the tank got hit with an armor piercing round, the shrapnel from the explosion would end my precious young life. All agreed. Experiment over. Tank removed.

Combat innovations often come from an idea someone had in the field of combat. Many suggested innovations come from the military suppliers like the one just discussed. Some though were well thought-out solutions to serious problems. Such was the ACH-47 Chinook gunship.

Of all the strange experiments performed in the crucible of Vietnam's battlefields an elite unit of Chinook Helicopter aircrews may take the record for the most bizarre. Unlike many of Vietnam's field experiments this one was commissioned by the Army. This unique combat experiment's short history was gallant but incredibly catastrophic. They called themselves, "Guns a Go Go."

The Chinook or CH-47 helicopter is a large, twin-engine,

My War with Vietnam

twin-rotor heavy lift machine. After several decades of service, it is still the Army's primary troop and supply aircraft. It is capable of flying enormous loads safely into very high altitudes. Its cavernous, fifty-foot-long cargo bay can carry forty armed troops. It can then re-supply these same troops on the next sortie with a ten-ton load of ammunition, food and medical supplies.

In the mid-sixties four massive Chinook helicopters were designated and re-configured for gunship work. They carried rocket pods, mini-guns, 40mm grenade launchers, 20mm cannons and several M-60 and 50 caliber machine guns.

Legends surrounding the aircraft began almost immediately.

In May of 1967 "Cost of Living" was lost horrifically when the mounts securing the 20mm cannon loosened in flight allowing the gun to fire at and destroy the ship's own forward rotor. On a gun-run at the time, there would be no recovery. The ship tumbled to its destruction carrying all of its aircrew members to their deaths.

Then on February 22, 1967, the two remaining gunships were engaged in intense fighting during the Battle of Hue. "Birth Control" took heavy fire, was shot down but managed a soft crash landing to a spot just 600 yards outside the Citadel. Risking everything, "Easy Money" settled down in a position between the burning aircraft and the enemy guns. The ship provided suppressing fire for its sistership and the only chance for the downed crew to be rescued.

Over-grossed on take-off, "Easy Money" took several hits and several crewmen were wounded. As the NVA commander had long hated these aircraft for their wicked, devastating air support, he offered a special reward to any soldier bringing one of these ships down. The enemy walked mortars up to "Birth Control" and destroyed the airplane on the ground.

The ACH-47 gunship typically carried in addition to fuel, crew and guns, three tons of ammunition. Its ability to loiter on site and offer devastating rocket and gun cover for ground troops endeared it to any grunt ever pinned down by enemy fire.

What set these gunships apart aside from being extraordinarily large, was their armament and the enormous load of ammo and fuel

Vietnam First Tour, Combat Assaults

they could carry. The early Huey gunships, a contemporary of the ACH-47, sometimes carried mini-guns and rockets. However, on a normal gun-run this smaller aircraft could only provide ground troops with brief air support. Normally they could only carry ammunition for just a few one- to two-minute bursts of deadly accurate streams of mini-gun fire.

Chinook gunship pilots sat in armored seats, for the most part safe from all but direct hits. Many critical engine, fuel and transmission parts were armor-protected as well. The ACH-47 carried an M5, 40mm grenade launcher in the nose. It also had a fixed 20mm forward firing cannon directly under the pilots. It had pods on the stubby "wings" on either side aft of the pilots that were armed with either 2.75 rockets or mini guns.

These behemoth gunships were configured for two door-gunners per side manning either M-60's or .50 cal. machine guns. There was also a door-gunner situated on the aft ramp with, usually, another .50 cal. machine gun. It took a crew of seven to fly and man this menacing airplane with all its guns. This array of firepower allowed for a 360-degree field of offensive fire. This is a tactical advantage neither today's gunship helicopters nor the "Spectre" AC-130 fixed wing gunship of the U.S. Air Force have.

After rigid testing by the Boeing company three of these airplanes were sent to Vung Tau, Republic of Vietnam for field testing. This small experimental unit with the big guns performed admirably in combat. The ships drew the admiration of flight crews and grunts alike. The first three individual ships into combat were christened with names: "Easy Money," "Stump Jumper" and "Birth Control."

The fourth aircraft, "Cost of Living," was sent to Edwards Air Force Base California for further evaluation. It would join its sister ships six months later in Vietnam when "Stump Jumper" was lost in a ground taxiing accident.

Decades after its 1956 development the only significant improvement besides a new suite of avionics, is the retrofitting of more powerful engines. Boeing Aircraft still makes this helicopter for several foreign countries.

My War with Vietnam

So much for the ghoulish but effective machinations of helicopter war. It doesn't speak though of the people who lubricate this machine, often with their lives. It does not tell of the human aspect.

It doesn't speak at all about the intense trauma and extraordinary demand on human capabilities. It says nothing of fear, courage, camaraderie, love, hate, confusion, and frustration, all inextricably knotted together, then stretched taut in a teenaged boy fighting a futile war he believes in less and less every day of his tour.

It says nothing of the faceless names who ordered the battles fought. Or the nameless faces who fight them.

The term "combat assault" means many things to me. Even now, years later, it means a young pilot I knew who, trapped in his downed aircraft, went insane watching his crew being deviously and horribly tortured by the Viet Cong.

It means at least one of my flight school classmates dying a hero's death. Shot down he had successfully pulled his copilot out of their downed and burning aircraft. He then deliberately went back for his crewmen.

He knew the danger. He knew the ship would blow up. Had to.

A downed Huey blows up three times. First the fuel explodes. Then the magnesium parts of the transmission explode in a separate white-hot blast. Then, seconds later, all the ammunition explodes or "cooks-off." Every pilot knows this three-step progression which invariably follows when a Huey begins to burn. And his ship was already burning.

He had dragged his copilot out of range, and they were safe. His copilot told me later Pete just looked at the burning wreck, shook his head, said, "shit!"

He then deliberately ran back into the inferno to get his crew dying with them in the explosion.

I think of times of my own incredible dread, flying over reported radar-guided .50 caliber positions. There had been no other route available due to deteriorating weather conditions. Or the time when flying as copilot on "Smokey" that our crew chief was killed and door gunner wounded, all within sixty seconds.

Vietnam First Tour, Combat Assaults

It means flying a Huey at 110 miles an hour 2 to 4 feet off the ground, pulling slightly up and flipping it sideways, 90 degrees to the earth, to get through a narrow tree line. This maneuver minimizes your "exposure time"—that is, time available as a target of hostile fire. This exposure time did increase if you slowed to gain altitude. But flying sideways for even a few seconds with the main rotor blades just clearing the ground was bravado. Folly.

An aspect of military flying is constant training. Helicopters are complex aircraft. We were always training on emergency procedures. There was a myriad of things that could go wrong with a Huey but seldom did.

One part of combat flying was breaking in new copilots. Copilots fresh out of Army flight school serve an apprenticeship. In the 116th we changed copilots every day so they could learn from the hopefully vast reservoir of knowledge, nuance and instinct for survival you as AC had accumulated.

In this unit when you were up for Aircraft Commander, all ACs in your platoon had to vote your approval. We had to absolutely trust each other flying tight formations under fire. One dissenting vote from any Aircraft Commander killed your chances to become an AC. Some pilots with less than a unanimous vote had to go to another platoon in the company. Some left the 116th altogether.

One day I'm flight lead of a two-ship sortie landing at a fire support base to pick up infantry. There were two pads side by side so we would come in together. After picking up six American troops for an extended stay in the boonies we would take off single ship, one at a time, then form up in the air.

These troops had a lot of gear, rations and ammunition. Saw one with his puppy. Twice I had picked the bird up, cleared the concertina wire at the edge of the compound, turned left over a river, into the wind, and nursed the bird into flying to gain altitude.

Third time I gave the controls to my new copilot, "You have the aircraft." He brings us in fine, empty. The troops get on board; he lifts off, clears the wire and shocked me by immediately turning right, downwind right over the river.

My War with Vietnam

As a heavy aircraft this is a catastrophic mistake. All airplanes need to take off into the wind, it adds lift to rotors or wings. Trying to take off going downwind deprives needed lift. I quickly grabbed the controls and per protocol said, "I've got it." But he froze on the controls. The next thing I hear on the radio is the second helicopter yelling my call sign, "Three-Three, your skids are in the water!"

I nursed the heavy helicopter downwind and upstream for quite a while, trading airspeed for altitude. I was also always fighting with my copilot for control yelling at him to take his hands off the controls.

I remember vividly the troops sitting in the cargo bay with their feet hanging out the cargo bay just clearing the water. With all their gear if we had crashed into the river they would drown. Stupid way to die in combat.

Finally, we're at 1500 feet and relatively safe he finally lets go and says something inane like, "Well, we did it." Not much given to profanity I remember lacing into him with language envied by stevedores worldwide. I ended by saying he would never fly with me again. And, if I could manage it, he'd never fly again in this unit or this war.

Shutting down that night my crew chief told me he had his 45-caliber automatic pointed at the back of the lieutenant's head. All I had to do was say the word.

He knew how much trouble we were in and was willing to kill to save us. Surprised he didn't.

Months later I was now flying the Four Star and a beat up, shot up, patched up 116th Hornet ship flew into the pattern at Saigon's heliport, designated Hotel-Three. Either the tower or another crew member would always let me know about a Hornet in the pattern. Because usually it meant the 116th crew had come to tell me one more of my friends had bought it.

This time though was different. That lieutenant was up for his vote. I won't divulge his name, but one hopes he never went into aviation as a career. Even though I wasn't officially an AC in that unit anymore they wanted me to vote because of that one mission I flew with him.

Vietnam First Tour, Combat Assaults

Without my crew I flew General Abrams' shiny new helicopter alone up to Cu Chi that night. Good to see everybody of course but the trip wasn't necessary. Wasn't necessary as half the other pilots voted against him. He left the unit.

There was also one of the single ship "Nighthawk" missions I flew, resupplying troops out in the jungle after dark. I wish I could truly describe night flying in Vietnam. It's still the only pure black I've ever seen.

Night was unaltered by any manmade light. In clear weather the horizon started where the stars stopped. Now take man's normal fear of the dark, add childlike imaginings of predators and hideous monsters living in the dark, awaiting prey. Then add one very young pilot trying hard for an elusive navigational fix and you have the ingredients giant fears are made of.

The predators and monsters are real down there in the dark. If your engine quits, they will own you forever.

Tuning in various radios searching for a fix that night I turned in the Armed Forces Network playing The Doors' "Light My Fire." The needle pointed to the station in Saigon giving me direction. I was found again. The hair on the back of my neck stood straight up when I heard that song. It was music from home, California, late sixties. Years later, starting instantly with the one beat, snare drum introduction, the first few bars of the song still give me chills. Still.

One dark night though also flying Nighthawk, I had a pleasant surprise. At flight school we often had to watch training films. Fly all day then ground school. One night at Fort Rucker in class the bulb burned out on the old film projector. We were sent back to the barracks for the night. Next night the instructor begins the class by announcing in his thick southern accent, "We're gonna watch a fim tonight if the bub don't bun." No L's or R's in his statement.

Toward the end of flight school with a wash-out rate of 50 percent there was maybe only ten of us or so in the class that night. But with a what-are-the-odds caveat, one of the other guys in my class that night was flying Nighthawk for another unit in the area. Guard frequency is always on. Listening for trouble every other aircraft in

My War with Vietnam

the air that night heard what I did. It was a perfect rendition of that instructor's voice, "We're gona watch a fim tonight if the bub don't bun." Had to smile.

I left combat flying on a fluke. Met a guy from my hometown, Pasadena, California, my first real day off towards the end of my tour with the 116th. Bumped into him my first visit ever to the USO in downtown Saigon. Neither of us knew the other was in the Army or was a pilot or in Vietnam. As I walked through the door he was lining up a pool shot facing the entrance.

He looked up over his pool cue, saw me and said, "What the hell are you doing here Jellerson?" "Flying with the 116th," I replied.

He said, "Gotta get you out of there or your mom will never forgive me." And made his shot.

I had so little understanding of things military I was amazed when a couple days later the second in command of the 116th, came to my hooch and said, "I don't know who you know, but you are out of here. You're ordered to Saigon to fly a two-star general. Pack your things."

Second Tour, Flying Generals and Movie Stars

I flew for two generals. The first was two star General Walter Richardson, the then military governor of Saigon, responsible directly to and only to President Nixon. Richardson was a wonderful mad man who loved to fly low and fast, leaning out the open side of the ship, allowing the wind to blast through his sparse, white hair.

Vern Estes was the detachment commander for the five pilots and crews and barely a friend then. But strangely, over the last forty-plus years he has proven to be one of my best friends. When I learned that General Richardson and Captain Curtis were both headed home I told Vern I wanted to transfer back to the 116th Assault. That bond developed in combat was so strong I felt certain I needed to get back there and serve alongside my brothers in arms. Vern spent two or three days talking me out of going back there. "If your friends in the 116th had a chance to get out they would. You're out. Unharmed. Stay out of it."

Might have saved my life too with all the KIA losses and wounded the 116th saw. General Richardson however had already called General Creighton Abrams, the military commander in Vietnam, in charge of all forces, all action and all other Generals. The respect between these two general officers was such that Richardson I heard, simply told him I should be his new pilot.

I was twenty-one years old.

My War with Vietnam

Two days after he made that call I took over as Aircraft Commander on the highest profile mission for the highest-ranking officer in the theater. Didn't see any paperwork. Didn't know until I finally went home much later that the FBI had investigated me for a top-secret clearance. Trolled the family and neighbors about me. I didn't know and wouldn't have cared anyway. My job was flying the man in charge. As such I was privy to some treasured but brief conversations. General Abrams was quite a man and a great general.

His career had gotten an early boost while he was a young colonel commanding a tank battalion during the Battle of the Bulge, World War II. I admired him.

One of the most common missions I flew for "Abe" was that of picking him up at MACV headquarters and dropping him onto the roof heliport of the U.S. Embassy in downtown Saigon. Military Assistance Command Vietnam or MACV was the overall power and decision maker for the entire war. As a writer I'm given to choosing my words carefully. I've heard it called the Vietnam conflict. Nope. Trust me, it was war.

I never went into the embassy. We were on instant standby alert on the roof top pad. Back at Hotel Three we were on fifteen-minute alert all day. Preflight the ship early morning and wait. By the time I left Vietnam I knew for a fact there were three things I would not do for a living. Even as much as I love flying I wouldn't become a VIP or corporate pilot, too much waiting around. I wouldn't go into medicine like much of my family. Too many medevac missions with too much blood and horrific wounds.

And I wouldn't fly crop dusters. Of the 700-plus combat hours I have from that time I'd bet two to three hundred were low level, skids barely clearing the foliage. That's enough.

Down below Abe would meet with Ambassador Bunker for hours. That heliport was mine. I would shut the ship down and wait for him. Ultimately, his aide-de-camp, then a very cool Colonel Noel, would radio, "Crank it up!" We'd start the ship. Abe would appear top of the stairs, walk to the aircraft and plug into the intercom. Every time before he or the aide would tell me where we needed to go next the General would plug in and say, "God damn politicians got my hands tied."

A direct quote. Every time he met with Bunker.

Heard that statement in my sleep for a couple years after leaving the Army.

While it was only an unsettling indictment then, in hindsight, it is awesome and terrifying.

Like Westmoreland before him, he had a plan to end and win that ugly war. But he was only a military man. The course of this painful American episode and many others as well would be decided by our trustworthy elected officials.

Our great Constitution with its separation of powers fortunately keeps America from becoming a Banana republic where militaries make up their own missions. But most politicians are neither gifted, trained or even remotely talented at conducting wars. They should just tell the military leadership what the objective is and get the hell out of their way. Our professional high-ranking, military leadership have both studied war and experienced combat.

Likely we will never know how many Americans have died in our many wars because of inept, unqualified politicians making critical decisions about how a battle should be fought from thousands of miles away.

What comes to my mind first happened during the Vietnamization phase of the war. During that time there were "No Fire Zones" established where if we took fire, we weren't supposed to shoot back ... believe it or not ... without getting permission.

Again, we were the only force over there with dark green American-made Bell helicopters. Shooting at one of our helicopters simply couldn't be "Friendly Fire." There was never a time or place over there when someone shooting at me when flying could be misconstrued. Only my enemy would do that.

More recently the Trump and Biden administrations both shamed our country around the entire world for their handling of our exit from Afghanistan. Trump set it up to fail with his agreement with the Taliban and Biden let it happen. The day Trump stated the

My War with Vietnam

date for the draw down he should have set up an office to do only two things.

First, issue visas to those Afghan citizens whom we promised we would protect for their service to us. And second, issue boarding passes to those same people so we would know how many aircraft would be required to fly them all out ... before the military left. And Biden should have insisted those two things were done before he sent our military home. Shameful.

The only good I can see from this disgraceful episode is in the future when a country is facing a civil war with dissidents or insurgents from within or attacked by their neighbors, they won't ask for our help. Countries around the planet have now seen how ineptly we prosecute our wars.

And how shamefully, we don't keep our promises.

Iraq and Afghanistan, two long wars in a row without an endgame or exit plan throwing money and American youth down the drain. We dishonor ourselves. Bush had a couple of years to end it. Obama had eight years to end it and Trump had four.

Flying General Abrams was worse than combat in a way. Good, proud duty of course, and much safer. I was aircraft commander on the highest profile helicopter mission in-country. After watching teenagers wounded and dying nearly every day on my first tour, my combat days were over.

But now I had more time to think. And much more troubling information to hear and digest.

The VIP pilots and crews were attached to the 120th Assault Company in Long Binh, "The Deans" for pay and maintenance. Vern and I didn't see eye to eye at first. Neither of us could have guessed that we would become great lifelong friends. I was a twenty-year-old hot shot pilot right out of a combat unit and a bit of a smart ass to boot, he told me.

Vern was a thirty-five-year-old senior cwo-3 ma (CW-3) and in charge of the VIP flight operation at Hotel Three. Hotel Three was aviation speak for heliport three. It was the heliport nearest

Second Tour, Flying Generals and Movie Stars

downtown Saigon just on the border of Ton Son Nhut Air Force Base. Now of course, Saigon has been renamed Ho Chi Minh City.

Vern was also Aircraft Commander on the second in command of the theater under General Abrams, General Wyand. I knew Vern but the first month or so we didn't interact much as I was copilot on General Richardson's Huey. We were stationed there with the Four Star's two aircraft. But the Aircraft Commander on the Two Star's Huey was Captain Don Curtis, my acquaintance from Pasadena.

Life was good that second tour. The best restaurants in Saigon were only a terrifying ten-minute Cicalo ride away. These motorized three wheeled taxis were everywhere. I was certain that the goal and ingenuity of having passengers sitting in front of the driver was we were to be the crash zone for the seemingly inevitable wreck. Rides could often generate as much adrenaline as flying into a hot LZ. And significantly more so in the latter case as we were at least in control on those combat missions.

The Cicalo driver could easily be a communist sympathizer ready and willing to take out a couple American pilots. There were bounties offered the Viet Cong guerrillas for killing American aircrews, particularly pilots.

Saigon should have been beautiful and maybe it once was. It had a great deal of French influence, particularly in its architecture. Beautiful wide streets with large roundabouts at many intersections. An abundance of natural foliage of course as the city was built on the banks of the Saigon River with flowers everywhere you looked.

But it was never built for the 3.3 million people living there in 1970. These roundabout traffic circles often looked like the chariot races from "Ben Hur." Cars, horse drawn carts full of produce or fish, Cicalos, bicycles and pedestrians all converging at once vying for space, forcing their way into position to get around the circle.

The black markets in Vietnam were infuriating. Picture a small stand like you might find in a flea market. On a Saigon street corner with a little canopy and goods displayed in cascading shelves, a young Vietnamese businessman is in charge. The goods for sale

My War with Vietnam

aren't fresh produce or fine silk or fish or flowers or the local jewelry like the other stands.

Displayed for all to see are Army issue Nomex flight gloves, Army issue pilot's sunglasses and more Army issued equipment. All these goods were supposed to be sent to the aviation units waging war only a few minutes away. Those units were out there making sacrifices and losing their lives daily allegedly for the independence of South Vietnam. It was my first introduction to the graft and corruption that existed behind the scenes in that war. Can't say for sure but I bet this likely takes place in every war.

Those responsible at the street level had to be condoned and supported likely by some top sergeant and his higher ups. Can't imagine how far up the chain of command it went. And I don't think I really want to know. But anyone traveling through the streets of Saigon could see it. They weren't hiding in dark alleys. They didn't open for business only after dark. This was a capitalistic enterprise in broad daylight.

Everyone knew, had to know. Why it existed and was not only allowed but protected by the Vietnamese police, the White Mice as they were called, is not a mystery. Everyone was getting their cut I'm sure. Corruption was rampant and pervasive, through the chain of command there. My own broad chain of command had to be involved somehow. Had to be.

La Cave was a restaurant in downtown Saigon while the beautiful floating restaurant on the Saigon River was only a block away. Both offered fresh lobster and excellent seafood dinners and some fine French wine for around ten dollars American. Fortunately, I didn't go there the night the floating restaurant was famously bombed.

When a movie star, head of state or a high-ranking officer from an ally came into town, Abe would turn his aircraft over to them. My crew and I went with the aircraft of course. These missions allowed me to meet quite a few pro football players, movie stars and starlets on USO tours.

I actually flew Stanley Resor, George Peppard, Vice President

Second Tour, Flying Generals and Movie Stars

Spiro Agnew, and many more. The only people I didn't fly were the President and Bob Hope. Those two brought their own crews. Peppard was interesting. He had just learned to fly to do the film "The Blue Max." One of the era's big stars just wanted to talk flying with other pilots. All of this quite the education for a twenty-one-year-old kid.

Flying the general had its moments. One day, taking him to the embassy rooftop I came in from a different direction because of a shift in the wind. Usually when landing at the embassy he would be seated on the right side of the ship. Getting out he would walk at a 45-degree angle off the nose of the ship and head for the stairs. He always had a lot on his mind and that day was no different.

As a creature of habit, he got off the ship and started walking at a 45-degree angle toward the edge of the heliport ten floors up. Rolling off RPM and studying gauges I happened to look over the instrument panel and saw him heading for the edge of the building. I yelled at my crew chief to go get him. Never forget the fascinating visual of my big crew chief grabbing the general by both shoulders and walking him back around the ship to the stairs.

Years later I would meet his son, another Army general, Creighton Abrams, Jr. He wanted to hear war stories about his dad. Nobody ever shot at Abe. So, I told him about the embassy rooftop episode. I added, "Your dad was so tough if he had walked off the helipad he'd likely just land hard, dust himself off and walk in through the bottom floor to meet with the Ambassador."

Once I had to fly Abe up to some good-sized base for a ceremony of some sort. A few miles out I could see a thunderstorm hovering right over that base. I told Abe we might have some difficulty landing for the extremely heavy rain. And there was no instrument landing system at this particular field. Of course, as I write this I feel compelled to clarify, I never called him Abe to his face, just sir or general.

He asked if we could circle a while and see if it clears. I did of course but it didn't improve. After telling him the bad news he replied with, "Then take us back home Mr. Jellerson. I didn't want to go to that goddamn ceremony anyway!"

My War with Vietnam

When General Abrams went to Thailand to be with his family or the U.S, for meetings, I was free to do whatever. One time I went to Thailand with him in his fixed wing, per VOCO, "Verbal Orders of the Commanding Officer." Sometimes I'd just take the ship and crew and go sightseeing or visit the 116th. A couple of times I'd leave the crew at the field and take the ship by myself and just go flying. Amazing to have that freedom and I'll take a moment to thank American taxpayers for that privilege. But really it was about staying proficient, a military mandate you understand.

As aircraft commander on General Abram's Huey, I was an anomaly. The VIP detachment flew the two four-stars in charge of the war. We were five pilots and two crew chiefs and door gunners for our two helicopters. The duty assignment was meant for senior Army pilots, master aviators, officers ready to go home after three combat tours and maybe even ready for retirement.

I was a fluke at twenty-one years old with only a couple thousand hours. As a matter of fact, the other four pilots called me "Boy." Had no problem with that nickname as I was in awe of the experienced, high time pilots I flew with.

I learned much from the other pilots, especially Vern. Attached to the 120th we had a problem with the commanding officer there. He had served in the Army for quite a while as he was a major before he went to flight school. So as a major he has to be in command of something. But as a new untested pilot without combat experience, why give him command of a helicopter company?

Interesting story involving Colonel Noel. Mornings, he would call me to discuss our missions that day. If we were to fly that day, he would tell me we are taking Abe to the Embassy or wherever else he wanted to go. One morning he called about flying the general to the embassy. But the local winds were such I told him we couldn't fly the rooftop pad. High winds burbling over the roof edge ten floors up could be hazardous. His cool response, "Okay, we'll drive."

But the major then commanding the 120th Aviation Company heard about me refusing to fly the general's mission. The major flew down and got me into the little waiting lounge we built, "locked my

Second Tour, Flying Generals and Movie Stars

heels" (had me come to attention) while he berated me for refusing to fly General Abrams. He said, "Your job is to fly the general."

My response directly back into his face only inches from mine, "Actually sir, my job is to fly that general ... safely!"

The next day Colonel Noel locked that major's heels right in front of me, again in our lounge. He lashed into him telling him, "Don't ever tell Mr. Jellerson how or when to fly. General Abrams likes how he flies." There was more.

Later, Vern told me that a superior officer is never supposed to dress down a lower grade officer in front of anyone with an even lower rank. The entire show was for my benefit.

That same major with no experience in-country once flew down to tell us our general's missions were so important we were to pre-fly them the day before. Vern told him, "No, sir, won't happen." The illogic and potential devastating consequences of doing that had eluded the major.

(From left) Don Curtis, myself and Paul Mac Michaels, all general's pilots (photo by Vern Estes, author's collection).

My War with Vietnam

Vern explained that everyone in Vietnam especially the enemy knew to whom those two shiny new Hueys out there belonged. Pre-flying a mission would allow the enemy to set up on our approach the next day and shoot us down. The major ran up against Vern again later when he decided that we should get two brand new helicopters every 100 hours. He was firmly told we didn't even have all the bugs worked out of them until around 300 hours. End of discussions with the major.

I also learned that junior officers are never supposed to prank senior officers, especially generals. But it happens.

Our detachment had a fixed-wing and crew equivalent across the base. The fixed-wing flight crew had a beautiful twin engine Beechcraft at their disposal. This aircraft was used for longer in-country flights out of range for our Hueys. We knew the other pilots of course. When time permitted, we gave each other stick time as all of us were dual rated.

I forget which general they were flying one day but well into one flight things took a strange turn. The night before, the pilots and copilots had gone to the officer's club and filled a paper bag with empty beer cans. At 12,000 feet or so the general was in back reading a report. There was a partition between the pilots' seats and the cabin with an opening for the aisle.

Suddenly, an empty beer can rolled and clanked down the aisle toward the general.

A moment later the pilots released another empty on a journey down the aisle to the general. I'm told it took four or five empties before the general even reacted.

Calmly, knowing he was being pranked, he paid them back in a most civil but never-the-less painful way. He went forward to the cockpit, returned their empties and without even acknowledging the prank or scolding them, gave them a new destination. Mid-flight, this is not easy. It requires a total reconfiguring of the flight plan. As they finished the new course and artillery clearances requiring several new calculations and radio calls, they promptly informed their passenger.

Second Tour, Flying Generals and Movie Stars

The general promptly then continued changing the destination again and again and again. At one point, suggesting they just put down at An Loc for ice cream. But whatever it takes to lighten up your day in war...

As professional and experienced as the VIP detachment pilots were, it wasn't always without problems. One day Vern was flying his general out to a fire support base. It's the rainy season with low clouds and often poor visibility. He thought he was close to the outpost and saw what pilots call a "sucker hole" in the clouds. That's an opening between clouds big enough to see the ground. You can dive down and see where you are and if you've done your dead reckoning navigation right you should see your desired destination.

The reason it earned the name sucker hole is because you might not be where you thought you should be. And Vern had indeed made a mistake. They weren't anywhere near the outpost. He had to explain to his passengers they had made a mistake and fly out of there fast as there could easily be an enemy below. The general had him fly back to MACV and report to him at the end of business that day. Before meeting with the general, Vern called a friend over at Air America saying he might need a job by tomorrow.

He went to see the general in his office armed with maps of the area so he could explain the mistake. After going over the day's flight path the general said, "So basically you were lost and flew us into an area unknown to you. Which means we could have been shot down."

Vern's response: "Yes sir. And I hope had that happened I would have been killed in the crash because the bullshit wouldn't be worth living through." We heard from Vern and the general's aid the general simply said, "See you in the morning Mr. Estes."

Flying General Abrams was an honor and quite the education for a 21-year-old. Vern told me and my family later several times that I was the most natural pilot he had ever flown with. As he went on to fly professionally until his retirement, I consider this another cherished compliment.

The FAA coined the term "Cockpit Resource Management" (CRM) recently. It means all input from the copilot and whomever

My War with Vietnam

else is in the cockpit is welcome to the captain, pilot in charge or as the military refers to it, aircraft commander.

I tapped into CRM on my second tour in 1970.

The Army has a hard and fast rule that the aircraft commander is the only one on board in absolute charge. If I say, "You have the aircraft" to my copilot he takes the controls and says, "I have the aircraft." I acknowledge his statement with a "You have it" and raise my hands in the air to underscore the change. In reverse I can say, "I have the aircraft" and the copilot says you have it and raises his hands.

A copilot would never tell the AC, "I'll take it." That situation would violate all the rules of military aviation going back decades.

Every copilot I had on that tour outranked me and had thousands more hours in their logbook than I. One day I even had a two-star general fresh out of flight school as my copilot. He called me "Sir" all day. Kinda liked that.

Our heliport base, Hotel-Three was basically within the city limits of Saigon right at the edge of the huge Tan Son Nhut Air Force Base. There are only two ways to cross an airport's-controlled airspace in an aircraft not intending to land there. With the tower's permission an aircraft can fly over the airport directly over the midpoint of the field or tower at several hundred feet above the pattern altitude.

The other way is to fly "under the active." Fixed wing planes approach landing on a runway at an approximate 11- to 12-degree angle. On departure they take off normally at about the same angle. So, several thousand feet from the departure or approach end of a runway you can, with tower permission again, fly low level under the active. Departing or approaching aircraft will fly over you. In Los Angeles you will see aircraft flying low level "under the active" along the beach under the aircraft departing to the west at LAX.

We had dropped off the general and were flying back to our base. Flying under Tan Son Nhut's departing active I was getting landing clearance from our Hotel Three tower. All of a sudden my copilot shouts, "I have it!" and grabs the controls. I said, "You have it" raising my hands in the air. Didn't yet know why he had violated strict protocols. But I also knew he was a highly experienced, competent pilot and wouldn't have done so on a whim.

He's pulling in power and climbing as fast as he can. I look around the airspace and can't believe what I see. A South Vietnamese C-47 is coming straight at us. Clearing the departure end of the runway they retracted their landing gear and remained low level. As they passed underneath us, even over the noise of my ship, I heard their two powerful radial engines below. Then I heard my crew chief sitting behind his M-60 machine gun calmly ask on intercom, "Mister Jellerson, can I lace him?"

We could have had a mid-air accident only feet off the ground. My copilot begins to say, "There wasn't time to…." And I cut him off, "You were going to say there wasn't time to do anything but save our lives. You can't apologize for that."

One time though I simply took the Huey without the crew and flew out toward the ocean from Saigon. The area was called the Runsat. It was low lying and flat with streams and ponds, elephant grass and pussy willow looking plants. It was a swamp or bog looking thing formed I think by the Saigon River delta between Saigon and the South China Sea.

Most Army helicopter pilots get severe nose bleeds if they climb over 3,000 feet. But one day, just to truly understand the operational ceiling of a Huey, I took Abe's ship by myself to 12,000 feet over the Runsat. I was out of Ton Son Nhut's control area. Reaching the 12,000-foot altitude the word mushy came to mind. The cyclic was mushy, loose and approaching it felt ineffectiveness.

Didn't want to stay there so…

There was another maneuver you didn't learn in flight school. Only taught in Vietnam as a combat contingency. It was called the High Overhead Approach.

It was an expedient for landing at helipads next to fire support bases. It made no sense to have a nice casual, civilian style down wind, base and final approach stretched out over Charlie-held country.

My War with Vietnam

So, this approach would begin at 3,000 feet or more directly over the helipad. Flip the bird on its side at a ninety-degree angle to the earth. Now you're looking at the planet and directly at the helipad out the left pilot's door of the aircraft. Drop the collective, taking all pitch out of the main rotor. Bleed off rpm with the toggle switch on the collective to avoid rotor over speed. Pull back on the cyclic to make for a tight spiral and fly, almost fall, down directly over the helipad.

Doing it right meant corkscrewing the ship down, landing smoothly on the pad and sliding only a couple inches. I remember doing it perfectly only once, but always fun. I did hear from Ton Son Nhut tower on the way down though. On their radar the spiral was so tight it had to look like an aircraft in trouble. My response, "Nope tower, Dean 087 just practicing, thanks."

There was another thing this lonely area of III Corps was good for. When Abe turned the bird over to a USO tour we were at their beck and call. This usually meant air taxi service. But when we hauled pro football players in town to boost morale, they wanted action. They would bring their super-eight motion picture cameras and wanted to see the Huey put through its paces.

My door gunner and crew chief would aim their M-60s straight forward and with us flying low and fast, fire away at "targets" ahead. These flights were about the only time my crew got to fire those guns. To the uniformed, their home movies might look like they had gone on a gun team mission.

Also, and only the professional athletes again would want to see interesting or unusual maneuvers. My favorite was the Hammerhead Stall. With the ship straight and level at maybe a thousand feet of altitude and doing top speed you pull back on the cyclic, nose up and aim for the stars. As you climb you lose air speed. When you have lost all your forward air speed but are still nose high, the ship will stall and automatically roll to the left in the same direction as the main rotor and dive down. Don't know what they captured on film, but I always got a kick out of doing that one too.

Didn't like the required ceremony violating military aviation traditions. Mornings we would land at the MACV helipad near the

Second Tour, Flying Generals and Movie Stars

general's compound. His bulletproof limo would pull up and with the turbine at idle I would open my door, step out, come to attention and salute him. This violated the rule that no one salutes on the flightline of any airfield. There were more important things to worry about like spinning propellers and rotor blades.

And since we're discussing violations, General Abrams' return salute definitely did not meet up to Army protocol or regulations. He would take his right hand, put his cigar between two fingers, take it out of his mouth and with the cigar glowing in the breeze, return my salute.

The highest-ranking officer in-country ... who's gonna tell him?

The Philippine four-star general I often flew was a favorite of my crew and myself. He came from the family that owned San Miguel brewery. After flying him on an inspection tour or some other mission we would drop him at his pad. And every time, his aid would put a case of San Miguel Dark under the jump seat in back. A six pack for each member of my crew. And still my favorite beer.

After Vietnam, Vern was the only one I stayed in touch with from the war. For several years he tried to get me back into aviation. He would call from some foreign land where he had gone to fly, always for the highest bidder. One time he called from the Philippines flying crews out to offshore oil rigs. "Three weeks of flying then a week of R and R and the money's great!"

Next he might call from Iran. He had contracted with Bell Helicopters to train Iranian pilots how to fly Hueys. He called once on his way to the Marshall Islands going to fly for the Nuclear Energy Commission. They paid well and needed dual rated pilots, helicopter and fixed wing.

Once he asked if I would like to get checked out on the C-130. Pilots always want to fly the next biggest aircraft. So, yeah Vern, what's up? Johannesburg!

An intelligence agency had asked him to devise a plan to get the massive wealth in Johannesburg, diamonds and gold, out of the country. They were concerned the government there might fall and be replaced by a wealthy insurgent force.

My War with Vietnam

He also called one time to tell me about an easy money job. Two quick trips a night in a Chinook, the big twin-rotor cargo aircraft … and you don't even have to land! Slow and low over the LZ and your kicker just pushes pallets of supplies out the back ramp. Thought a minute and said, "The only place where that type of mission would be a fit right now would probably be Afghanistan, right?" "Right!" he replied happily. "And have you heard about the big nasty Russian Hind gunships over there?" "Oh, hell yes. I'm not an idiot. I wouldn't take that job. Just thought I'd run it by you."

He flew for the Alyeska pipeline among many others. A gifted professional flying bum.

His last post was chief pilot at Hanford Nuclear Energy in Washington State on the Columbia River. They had a small fleet of three helicopters almost always on patrol. From there he called to tell me, "Just pack and get up here. No check ride for you, I know how you fly." He explained after he retired as he was forbidden to disclose it before, that the ships also carried armed SWAT teams. Any incursion into the base would have been met with deadly force.

After he retired he began making models of, naturally, aircraft. He bought three same scale Huey helicopter models and spent two years building a Smithsonian museum quality model of the Huey I flew with the Hornets.

The detail was amazing. He put my actual tail numbers from my logs, put the ship in Hornet livery with the big white Hornet on the nose. The top of one main rotor was painted white as well, representing as being from my Wasp platoon. As the models had doors and the Hornets flew during the dry season anyway with no doors, he cut them out. Then created the interior complete with an instrument panel and comm wires hanging from helmets.

He called toward the finish of his work to ask me if I remembered the bullet holes in my aircraft. There were three never to be forgotten.

Over a hot LZ on final approach in the 116th one day, I felt a round hit us. With both feet on the pedals there was no mistaking that incredibly sharp tug on the pedals. Opening the tail rotor drive shaft inspection panel hours later at day's end was a shock. We found a deep, five-inch scar in the drive shaft. There was an armor piercing AK-47 round bent in a ninety-degree angle lying on the shelf beneath the shaft. The Bell tech rep told me that should have started a vibration in the drive shaft so severe it was capable of tearing the ship apart—and really, it should have.

Next day my crew chief was wearing that bent round as a necklace. Vern put that bullet hole with the appropriate patch on the model.

I was asked once who was my first love? Thought about it and said, "I dated several girls before the Army but nothing serious. My first love was a Huey."

No, really. Flying into an LZ you can both hear and feel the aircraft taking hits. Drop the troops off, add power and that beautiful, wounded machine flies you right back out every time. It did me anyway.

I prefer flying helicopters from the right seat, aviation tradition aside, as the pilot in command or aircraft commander usually takes the left seat. Had to fly left seat for the Four Star. But at the 116th I took one round just over my head in the frame of the right door flying one day. Vern got the bullet hole and the patch right again.

Then there was the third memorable bullet hole. Happened in my chin bubble right between my feet on the pedals. Flying Smokey one day in the 116th following Stinger lead in, I took the hit. Immediately calling Stinger gun team lead to state I was taking fire. Quite sure my voice sounded a couple octaves higher than normal. Before Stinger lead could even respond I heard my crew chief on the ship's intercom. "Mr. Jellerson sir, that wasn't incoming, it was outbound!" "What?" "Shit!" "How?"

The smoke ship often on very hairy missions had the normal door gunner and crew chief with their mounted M-60s of course just like the slicks. But we would also add what we called a roving gunner. The extra man would have two unmounted M-60s and as the name suggests, would move to the side of the aircraft taking the heaviest fire and add to our outbound cover fire.

My War with Vietnam

After long extended bursts of fire the barrels of these machine guns could actually get so hot they would glow a dull red. My crew chief explained the roving gunner put his overheated M-60 on the cargo floor and picked up his other gun. The one on the deck of the ship was so hot a round cooked off and exited the aircraft right between my feet. I would have preferred, as counterintuitive as it sounds, that it had been an incoming round. Taking fire from your own cargo compartment just felt wrong. Vern got that hole and the patch right again.

I have a pretty extensive collection of extraordinary original art, mainly abstract and surrealist. I've been collecting from all over the world since I was twenty. But when Vern gave me that little piece of art and expression of his friendship it became my favorite. He came down from Washington state a couple times. We took some road trips and some off-road trips together. But he suffered some health issues later in life.

In 2023 he had to have heart surgery. I called one time to check on him and his wife answered his cell for him. I've learned through life as of late this is usually a bad omen. And I was right. His last surgery had not gone well. He was home but in hospice. His wife Toni said he was sleeping but she could get him up for me. I said no, let him sleep. But please have him call me when he's up to it.

Three weeks later I called again having not heard from him. This time she got him to call me back. He sounded weak. Not like my strong friend I had known now for fifty years. I could tell it was taking a lot out of him just to talk. Long pauses between sentences to catch his breath. They had taken him off his meds as there was no more that could be done. No saving him now.

He told me how important our friendship had been to him all these years. And it hit me, he was really calling to say goodbye. I have lost many immediate family members, cousins and friends these past years. But I have never been so moved, so touched or felt so loved. No one I lost ever had the opportunity to say goodbye to me. Nor did I ever have the privilege of saying goodbye to them except for Vern. Sad. I got him to laugh a bit reminding him how we really didn't get

Second Tour, Flying Generals and Movie Stars

along at first. And I too, said goodbye. Toni called a day or so later to tell me he was gone. I miss him.

I remember one time while in the Tan Son Nhut pattern returning to Hotel Three I heard a strange conversation between the tower, and what had to be a U-2 spy plane. The tower operator said sternly, "Aircraft at 60,000 feet identify yourself." The pilot's response was equally stern, "Get your god damned radar off me." Nothing more was said between them.

Batchelor officers quarters for the four General's pilots and the six gunship pilots was definitely outside the norm for the Army. We had a magnificent French mansion, mostly marble with walls all around it about ten feet high. The huge house was halfway between our heliport and downtown Saigon on a major boulevard.

Home sweet home with machine gun nests at each corner of the walls.

Earlier crews had created a home-built bar next to the fishpond in the yard. Can't even believe how many mornings the four of us VIP pilots on our way to preflight had to pull a couple of gunship pilots out of the pond. Passed out and slept there all night. Lucky they didn't drown. The rooms inside the palace were huge with fans in the ceilings and really high ceilings in the way people do in hot climates.

We had a mongrel dog with hair on its spine running the wrong way. Wasn't hair sprayed. It was a razorback mutt, the gun team's mascot. Never knew before then how much a dog could love beer. Usually handled it well too. Other times wobbly just like the pilots who gave him the beer.

I flew General Abrams out to a fire support base once for a ceremony of some sort. I stayed in the aircraft while he was driven back and forth to the occasion. When he arrived back we were already running and getting clearances to leave. The outpost's major was standing at attention a few feet away off the port side of the aircraft and holding his salute. I was embarrassed for him as the General was already on board talking to his aid. But there he stood in obeisance to the God-like Four Star.

My War with Vietnam

The tower had asked me to take off and depart at a 45-degree angle from the pad as there was traffic in the pattern. This departure would take me directly over the major. So, with exaggerated sign language over the roar of the helicopter I tried to show him what I had to do to leave. He didn't get it. As I lifted off directly over him, still holding his salute I saw his hat leave and his uniform get seriously messed up.

Most missions I flew for General Abrams were docile, gentlemanly flights. He never flew after dark. Liked him for that. When we left the city limits of Saigon we had the Razorbacks heavy gunship escort. Liked him for that too. A heavy gun team was three gunships while two gunships was deemed a light gun team.

There was also a single empty Huey flying "chase" following behind us. In the event I had an engine failure the plan was I would auto-rotate down, glide to the ground to a soft landing if I did it right the first time. Actually, as I may have mentioned, the first time was the only chance you had to get it right.

The plan for this turn of events was when we landed the General, his aide, my entire crew and I would run to the empty but running slick. All of us would jump on board and fly away with two of the three gunships. That other poor schmuck flight crew would stay with my downed, engine-out aircraft. One lonely gunship circling overhead. Drawing that chase mission had to suck.

I used my company call sign and aircraft tail numbers "Dean 087" in most radio calls to control towers and artillery clearances. But when Abe was on board, just like when the President steps on board Air Force One, we had a specific call sign. We became "Taskmaster 6." Amazing on final approach to airports and bases to see jeeps and officers running around trying to get ready for his arrival.

One day I flew the General and somebody from Washington, D.C., out to a large Navy ship well out into the South China Sea. The chase ship followed me in case we had to ditch but no gun team this time. We didn't figure we would run afoul of an enemy ambush over the ocean.

Second Tour, Flying Generals and Movie Stars

The big ship was rocking in heavy seas up and down, back and forth, not a still moment to be found. I had to set the aircraft down on the pitching deck somehow. The first few attempts didn't go well at all. But there had to be a rhythm to it, some sense of timing for the deck and helicopter to connect in symbiosis, in harmony, right? Nope, none I could find anyway.

Looking around it looked to me like the sailors were exchanging money up on the deck above the helipad. Had the feeling they were making bets on my successful or unsuccessful landing. Wonder what odds I was getting. Eventually I just hovered and waited for the deck to come to me. Simple really.

Then it happened one day. Time served. At the end of my second tour in country I had truly witnessed the Yin Yang of war. Horrific images would be seared into my consciousness forever. But it was over. I could go home now physically unharmed. Within three days of getting out and starting home, I was still in Saigon at our home-built bar. Both Air America and the Navy recruited me.

The Navy wanted to transition me into jets so they would have high-time dual rated pilots, rotary and fixed wing. Told the guy in the snappy Navy uniform no. Never regretted that decision until the movie *Top Gun* came out in the eighties.

Air America was the CIA's air force flying clandestine missions mostly in Laos and Cambodia over the Ho Chi Minh trail. Still don't regret telling them no.

First tour my ship was shot up but never shot down. Ask any pilot, a huge difference. Lost a lot of friends on my first tour, needlessly it turns out. A lot of good men lost their lives there. Didn't give their lives for this country, lost them. There is a difference. Ask someone in our military. Began to have an understanding as to why during my second tour I was hanging out with the brass.

When I told General Abrams I was getting out of the Army, he shook my hand and wished the best for me. He also wrote a letter about my service flying him. He later wrote a letter to help get me into law school. And his wife sent me Christmas cards every year until he died.

I left that country discouraged about human nature and troubled over our purpose and role in that war, and in general on this planet. Felt uncomfortable, disorganized and yes, tricked. Didn't feel like I was ready to go back to America. My country was deeply troubled and divided then. Protests ... some violent.

Seemed freedom of speech had turned into rather an ugly form of aggression. Opposing sides didn't seem to want to reconcile, just argue. Peaceful demonstrations often turned into ugly, angry riots. Neither side moved their cause or beliefs forward. These confrontations simply moved sides further and further toward hating and misunderstanding each other.

Yes, an eight-by-ten glossy of General Creighton Abrams autographed to me (Army Public Affairs, author's collection).

Have to say I wasn't truly reconciled yet with what I'd seen on my two tours either. The basest instincts of men are the daily palette on the canvas of war.

Why go back to another war zone?

The offered brotherhood gets you through the fighting. The healing you do on your own.

The Army wasn't going to fly me home anyway. For some reason they were obligated to fly me back to Hawaii where they had drafted me. So, instead of going straight home to Los Angeles, family and

Second Tour, Flying Generals and Movie Stars

HEADQUARTERS
UNITED STATES MILITARY ASSISTANCE COMMAND, VIETNAM
OFFICE OF THE COMMANDER
APO SAN FRANCISCO 96222

MACJOO　　　　　　　　　　　　　　　　　1 October 1970

CW2 Richard W. Jellerson,
Saigon VIP Detachment
120th Assault Helicopter Company
APO 96307

1. On your departure from Vietnam and separation from the United States Army, I wish to extend my personal appreciation for your service as Aircraft Commander and Pilot of my command and control helicopter.

2. Throughout your assignment to Headquarters, United States Military Assistance Command, Vietnam, I have been impressed by your professional attitude, technical skill, experience, and dedication. The standard of performance you set exemplifies the high quality of our country's young men who have willingly carried more than their share of the load in Vietnam.

3. I congratulate you on your accomplishments while in the United States Army and wish you continued success in the future.

CREIGHTON W. ABRAMS
General, United States Army
Commanding

I left the Army, the General wrote this letter (author's collection).

home, I bought a ticket on "Pan American Flight One." An amazing concept from the company who pioneered passenger aviation. This single airline ticket would take you around our entire world. The ticket was a magic carpet to the major cities or capitals of many countries around the planet.

The best part and a truly unique innovation was that the ticket

My War with Vietnam

was good for an entire year! It allowed you to get off and stay in a country as long as you wanted.

Then get back on the next Pan Am Flight One headed west. Calcutta, Istanbul, Tehran, Bangkok, Hong Kong, Berlin, London ... the World.

Spin the schoolroom globe. I went alone.

Thailand...

The first leg of the journey took me to Thailand. This very old country looked exactly like most of Vietnam from the air of course. It had intense green jungle, forested mountains and a huge system of tributaries and rivers. They all lead to the birth mother of all the early civilizations in Southeast Asia, the great Mekong River.

On a hot humid day, I was sitting in the shade at a small dirt strip airport outside Bangkok. This wasn't their municipal or international airport. A small, quiet breeze eased through periodically trying very hard to cool the afternoon. It pushed through a cloying sweet smell of flowers. Were they seen rather than smelled they would be purple. Such is the mental assessment of my mind trying to understand an undefined plant.

I was waiting for a small feeder line airplane, hopefully a twin-engine. Trying to get out to a rural village I was going to another dirt strip somewhere off into another part of Thailand. I would see this country first. It was a side trip, an exploration. I was to take many side-trips on this journey. I was exploring the world.

The Thai are a beautiful, gracious people. Most live and work in the cities. Many too then lived in beautiful homes built of pure teak on the many rivers that crisscross their country. These fortunate people go to work, school and markets by boat. It's a simple and, I imagine, splendid life with tight families living off the land and the fish they catch off their front porch.

At the small airport I met a young Thai girl, maybe in her teens.

My War with Vietnam

She was pushing a bright white wooden cart selling soft drinks and headed directly for me. Her beautiful, natural smile became her introduction as a merchant. After selling me a warm Coke the young girl sat on the bench next to me and offered to share her small lunch if we could just talk about America for a while.

This felt to me a strange and uncomfortable request. She surprised me and I wasn't ready to talk about it. I didn't want to. I resisted. Had to think about it. I had changed so much I didn't yet understand my feelings about America.

A feeling that bubbled often to the top though was that I had been betrayed.

Growing up in Southern California was a rich, textured childhood of friends and fun. Don't remember a contentious or otherwise uncomfortable day at school or anywhere else in my life. Life on cruise control. Made good money at some part time jobs in Pasadena. I had a beautiful white 57 Chevy coupe to cruise Colorado Boulevard and a couple dirt bikes. Between the beach, beautiful girls, the Mojave Desert with no speed limits, sandlot football and friends, life was full.

I was happy, content, fulfilled. Hadn't yet given thought to what I would do with my life. But didn't feel rushed to figure it out either. It would come to me.

I graduated from Pasadena High School and went directly to Pasadena City College for a while. I did get my junior college degree, but it wasn't easy. So many distractions. Blonde, brunette and redhead distractions were everywhere. Social life and my dance card were full. I went Grunion hunting at night with my friends on the beaches of Southern California. Cruised those same beaches next day meeting young women in bikinis. Took my dirt bike off-road on every trail and dirt road in the vast Mojave Desert behind the mountain range that forms the Los Angeles basin.

Young and healthy, I had known some of my good friends all my life so far. Assumed then we would all be life-long friends. Always in touch, always knowing we were there for each other. That was my always.

Thailand...

Didn't think I needed to see anything outside California. Didn't need to meet new people, explore new lands or leave the sublime mystique of Southern California.

Then the war. Life took a hairpin turn on what I thought was going to be a straight stretch of smooth highway ahead.

This young Thai girl was so sweet, I was captivated, enchanted. Her candor and honesty pulled me into her world and her questions. Those beguiling big brown eyes didn't hurt at all either.

The shelf under the commercial part of the cart held her entire retail inventory of seven to eight lukewarm sodas. Capitalism is flawed but amazing. Probably, if the cokes were even real, she bought them for 50 cents, and sold them for two dollars. She pulled out a sandwich wrap of Thai seafood. She split her meager lunch in two with her small brown hands and shared it with me.

Upbeat and positive she was sure she would go to America someday. Wanted to anyway. Wanted to attend one of our colleges. She wanted to know, "What's it really like there?" "Are there really parks, free schools, and skyscrapers and...?" On she went. Questions tumbled out of her like a spring rain.

Eventually I came to realize I could answer her questions and address her curiosity only when she took a breath, should she elect to ever do so. The plane was late, and we spoke for quite a while. She in broken English, me in "pidgin" English and some sign language. But it worked.

I was trying to remember what America was like. Scenes coming to my mind were like watching an old black and white television with periodic crackling, static laden losses of signal.

Our culture has done its best through movies and television to show us how life worked in fiction. Inane TV programs with likable families working their way through issues always ended well. Westerns portrayed gunfights. A cowboy on a barn roof would get shot, grab his stomach and say, "Oh, you got me" and fall behind the barn. Never saw a wound.

But in reality, bullets blow big, raggedy jagged holes in people. And there's blood everywhere.

My War with Vietnam

I wasn't quite sure how I felt about America just yet. I was entertaining thoughts of not going back at all. I was considering immigrating to somewhere else. First thought was Australia, but maybe Thailand.

I'm sure now that I was then brittle, perhaps broken inside, burnt out emotionally.

But somehow this gentle girl was touching me. Unknowingly she had prodded and probed at something I didn't yet understand.

America wasn't what she thought it was anyway was it? It certainly wasn't what I thought it had been. My country and I had both changed so much I wasn't sure we would recognize each other.

Didn't know if the American dream was still there at all. My perceptions were clouded, murky and obviously had not withstood the chaos of war. My view of life in America had eroded, shifted and changed.

I had been through an awful lot considering there were no visible scars.

Wasn't at all proud of what I'd seen in America on my brief leave there between tours in Vietnam. I also wasn't nearly reconciled with what I'd seen during either of my tours there."

Would I ever understand and embrace the changes in me and my country? The question seemed to loom on the horizon directly over an ominous cliff. There would need to be a reckoning if my life were to move on. And until I had answers there would be no healing. At least, it seemed that was the order of things.

Later I would understand this was not the way of things. Didn't yet know that I needed to heal before questions were answered for my life to move forward.

My jagged, war-torn psyche was somehow calmed and quieted by hearing a foreigner speak so lovingly about my country. Didn't yet know why her conversation stilled and soothed my senses, why it moved me the way it did.

Didn't know the journey I had yet to take. Didn't yet recognize I was even on a journey other than the one for which I had purchased an airline ticket.

Thailand...

Remaining stoic, appearing brave, internalizing everything you see and witness in combat may not be good for you. But there was no choice. So, you deal with the hand you're dealt. And this morass of suspicions, doubts, fears while witnessing the atrocity of war just festers inside.

Certainly, there was no one to come home to who asks, "How was your day, dear?" No counsel but a warm, flat beer at our shabby little officer's club if you didn't have a mission to fly that night. If you're having the same nightmare every night and every day, it's not a nightmare. It's real.

We talked easily until my plane arrived. Never knew her name. Didn't realize that hers were only the first hands to be outstretched to me. Traveling around the world she would only be the first to try and bring me back. Back to me. Back to being a functioning human again.

Further into the Thai outback with a truck and guide I came across a village. I had the sense the village had prospered happily in its own quiet way for centuries on that very riverbank. It had an open school, one classroom actually. There were no sides to the one story building but it had a metal roof. The only metal roof in the village.

Ten or so children from around nine to early teens were sitting on wooden benches. I wondered what they were learning.

There was a chalkboard with math equations on it. But what else would they need to survive out here? Fishing and hunting skills if they stay. Language and social skills if they move to an urban environment and plan to have a career in some "civilized" discipline.

Wonder what I could teach them? Wasn't asked to offer any insights anyway. Just felt I had learned so much I should share.

Share what, the horror of war? Humanity chewing away, gnawing barbarically at each other's bones. I'd rather these children didn't know that, never know that.

I couldn't have been the first Caucasian they had ever seen. But they stared at me anyway.

I know now I was on my way back, taking a complicated, troubled journey back to the human race. The journey I had just finished in war was complicated and troubled too. But now, with the unsolicited help of strangers, I had to find my way back home. Back to me, back to myself who had somehow been left behind. Hopefully, I was still out there, waiting, anxiously waiting for my own return.

Likely though the children saw my aura if you will. Had to be one of immersion in death, despair, loss. I was never sure if there were any visible manifestations of my inner disquiet. Perhaps people everywhere just pick up vibrations off troubled fellow beings.

All the children looked so happy, clean, healthy. Their youth reminded me of mine so very long ago. Could I have ever been that young, trusting, naive?

Hong Kong...

In a huge, sparkling clean theater near the harbor I sat surrounded by Chinese families watching "Airport" with Chinese subtitles. I'm the foreigner here.
I'm the minority. I'm alone in another peoples' land. They do not share their fears, secrets, biases, or bigotries with me.
Still war-torn I sit, quietly suspecting them of disliking me purely for my race. What a concept. Judged, cataloged and categorized by skin color. They should be better than that, right? Actually, they probably hadn't given me a thought.
I was conjuring up insecurities. Still as the families passed by after the film's end, many offered a smile. Only a courtesy perhaps. But maybe a message too, a welcome? Maybe only tolerance.
My unrest and discomfort I believe now was that I was still in an Asian country. Perhaps after combat with the Vietnamese I would always resent Asians? I didn't want that. Candidly, I could not, would not accept that. I wasn't raised to be a bigot or racist.
Raised by a single mom, a powerful warrior herself, she taught her kids we were no better than and no less than anyone else. She taught her children a lot more than self-worth. Told us, "Whatever you want, want to be, want from life—go get it!
I can't give it to you, and neither will anyone else."
Towards the end of her life as her oldest she confided in me. "I wished I could have given you more, done more for you boys." My

My War with Vietnam

brothers and I had lost our only sister in a car wreck years ago. Nearly lost Mom in the same accident.

My reply, "What you gave us is that we are healthy, happy and accept that we work, we play, we understand life. It doesn't get any better than that, Mom. You did good."

Poorly said perhaps, but forever grateful I had the chance to tell her that.

Didn't happen quickly but consciously I decided to get past this stumbling block to a life well lived. I willed myself to work my way through it. With mom's advice and a strong will, I would never be a racist.

Years later I knew I was okay when I became seriously involved with a beautiful Japanese woman. My Dad had issues with her as he was a World War II veteran. Shortly after he actually met her and got to know her though, he worked his way through it. Rather quickly I thought. Proud of him.

Saw the grand opening of the first McDonald's in Hong Kong. Cabbies and hotel staff told me they couldn't get the franchise open for a long time. No one thought it would work. The day it opened Chinese families lined around all four sides of a big city block. Good or bad, the planet was homogenizing.

My westward movement around the globe was away from the void of logic, the crucible of pain and self-doubt that is war. Still couldn't know how much I needed to move toward being re-embraced by humanity.

My tribe had left me to discover life ballistically. Not real life. War. Not how life should be lived on this planet. And growing up in America at that time did not prepare me for who I needed to be to get through Vietnam. Had I been raised in a climate of hate and fear I'm certain I'd have been better prepared for combat.

If I had grown up in a country in constant state of assault by outside aggressors, neighboring countries mostly, I would certainly be a different person. If I had always lived in a combat zone, my country at constant war for decades, I would likely be ready, easily accepting, indeed trained for my role in life. And since it had been my life

Hong Kong...

there would be no transition back to the real world. Likely no healing required.

Many of the young Vietnamese on both sides of this civil war were my age. They had been born into, grown up and lived at war their entire lives. I wonder how they viewed the war. After all, we were the invaders.

I had survived it. But what was needed now? What next?

The Star Ferry ride between Hong Kong and Kowloon always made me feel crowded but comfortable and tall. Crowded because we were. Not sure there was a load limit or lifeboats for all of us. Comfortable because I'd always felt at home on the water. Tall because literally I was around eight inches taller than everyone else on the boat. I was young and that seemed important.

Bought an Omega Speedmaster Professional chronograph watch, a pilot's watch. Beautiful craftsmanship, wearing it still today. But the original metal wrist band pulled the hairs on my wrist. So, I went back to the Chinese merchant next day.

He happily switched the steel wrist band to a cheap rubber one and kept the high-end band. Seemed to be enjoying the transaction with a big smile. It was days later on a flight out of Hong Kong's surreal airport when I figured it out. He had taught me a valuable business lesson. Early signs of how the world really works.

Lebanon...

ON PAN AM Flight One, as I remember, except for first class, seats weren't assigned. I like window seats. Pilots are control freaks and even as a passenger I must feed my need for situational awareness.

Leaving for Lebanon I pushed my overnighter into the overhead and looked out the port at the hustle of an airport's operations. Other passengers are boarding up the steps. All of us should be a little excited about air travel to a place we've never been. Some passengers though seem jaded to the whole process of beginning a journey. For them maybe the journey wasn't new, just a job. Coming up the aisle there are well-dressed, well-groomed businessmen in nice suits with turbans on their heads.

Right behind them though there's another guy coming up the aisle. Unlike the rest, kind of scruffy. Unshaven, unkempt, blue jeans, tee shirt, hunting vest, couple of cameras slung over his left shoulder.

He stops at my row. "Seat taken? You're American right? Hi, I'm Neal." There are only two luxurious, wide leather seats in a row. He jams his camera case in the overhead and drops into the aisle seat.

"Hi, Neal." That awkward turning to your side to shake hands is quickly over with. "Nice to meet you." "Looks like you're just out of Vietnam."

"Yeah, taking the long way home. How can you tell?"

"The haircut is a dead giveaway, Army. And nobody wears those

My War with Vietnam

shirts anymore. And the look." "The look?" I asked. "That deeply troubled, thousand-yard stare like, 'What's out there ahead of me?'"

"Great, can't hide." "Not from me anyway."

"What do you do?" I said. "I'm a photojournalist, war correspondent. A stringer."

I'm sure he saw a question forming on my face, so he continued.

"Means freelance. I have to find the story, document it and sell it. Post, LA Times, Time magazine once. Did get my byline out on a few stories about your war."

"Not my war anymore, thanks. I'm done. Out. What are you looking for?"

"In my line of work, you always need another conflict. Good to be first to get it, too."

We were loaded up. The ground crew wheeled the steps away from the plane. The stewardess closed the main door. Another was already taking drink orders and offering reading material, magazines. It's 1970. In-flight movies won't be invented for years to come. And would I like steak or fish for dinner tonight?

I asked Neal, "So you go around looking for wars?"

"Yep. You're headed out of a war, and I'm trying to find the next one."

"And where is the next one?"

"I think we're headed right into it. This part of the world has always been ripe for conflicts. Think there's another one brewing up ahead in Lebanon ... or nearby."

My new traveling companion cleared his throat as if making a presentation to his editor or a client, "See, the Jordanian government recently expelled the Palestine Liberation Organization. In no small measure this was done to end Israel's excuse for continuously raiding into, invading Jordan to fight the PLO. Even though Syria sent troops to aid the PLO, they were forced to move to Lebanon. At the least I'm expecting civil unrest, maybe even protests. It's how these always things start."

"Always?"

"Almost always. Rare when conflicts start with a declaration of

Lebanon...

war. Usually lots of accusing, screaming and finger pointing before any shots are fired."

"Great, war-starting has a formula. You know, someone said the definition of insanity is doing the same thing over and over but expecting different results. You'd think with war we would know better."

Neal is quiet for a bit. Then from a deep well of cynicism he says, "Can't get around human nature. We've been taking what we want or need from our neighbors since the Stone Age."

"And is that really human nature or learned behavior? We should be better than that."

Neal again goes quiet for a moment, fails to answer my question but says, "Hope you find what you need after this. Seen a lot of you guys all lost with thousand-yard stares, trying to figure life out after fighting.... Hell, life *is* fighting."

"Can't buy that." My beer arrived. I had yet to discover the grace and majesty of single malt scotch. "I think you might be even more cynical than I am."

"Probably am." Neal's drink arrived, "Been at it longer too. You're new at it. What are you, twenty years old? I've got about ten years on you."

The plane is being pushed back from the gate. The engines are spooling up one at a time. I ventured, "Do you remember?"

"Remember what? The change?"

I paused a moment, thinking. Was I asking him or myself? "Yeah, how'd you get so cynical, so negative about this life, our world?"

"I don't remember a day or certain incident when I changed or even that I had changed. Until I saw it in everyone around me. Seen it in all the kids they send to war like you. Like watching a match flare. Righteousness. Patriotism. All hot flame until you see how it is in the world. Then just blackened ash and smoke. Once it flares and gone to ash you can't relight it."

Pessimistic about the world ... life itself. Like a lot of people sitting next to each other on planes there are acknowledged times

My War with Vietnam

silence is okay, even a good thing. I didn't want to talk to him the rest of the flight. His was not a perspective I wanted to embrace.

But he's persistent, "You know why they prophesied the end of the world; Armageddon—will be here in the Middle East?"

I had thought about this before, "I think it's because this region then was the entire known world, the whole universe to any people who then had a language."

"Clever. College?"

"Yeah, and Sunday School. Doesn't matter the where. The dynamic is troubling. Why should there be a great conflict between good and evil? An end at all?" He yawns his response, "Sorry, but I'm tired. Been camping the last few days with an armored division right on the North Vietnamese border. As if they care about borders. I'm going to rest a bit."

Wonder if he's right about that match, my match not re-lighting? Hasn't for him obviously. But what about me? Am I as far-gone as he is? I know I'm not who I was but I'm too young to be a burnt-out hulk, down on life, negative about everything for the rest of my days.

On final approach to Beirut airport, I watched the gorgeous, shallowing Mediterranean pass beneath. I thought this next country would be a wonderful place to explore, so much history ... couldn't wait to see it. After landing and taxiing to the terminal I had a complete change of heart. Didn't even get off the plane. Sat in air-conditioned comfort and watched, horrified.

"Neal, wake up. I think you found your war."

Outside, racing through waves of heat undulating off the tarmac were Jeeps with mounted machine guns and armed soldiers. Everything I wanted to leave behind. Fear, tension, intimidation, unrest. I couldn't know then that this country would foment and sponsor terrorism. But certainly, this early trouble should have indicated a propensity for disruption and disquiet.

Grabbing his bag, Neal turns to head down the aisle. "Nice to meet you. Maybe we'll meet again, maybe not. But either way good luck to you." Shaking hands again, "Good luck to you too. No offense but I hope you're wrong about a war here and that life is just fighting."

Lebanon...

He gave me the saddest smile I've ever seen and walked off the plane.

Still in my seat, plane still waiting on the ground I felt a troubling and growing discomfort. What kept these young soldiers from just blasting away at this very vulnerable aircraft? Discipline? Orders? Who gave them orders? And the other side of the tension I felt, the angst in my heart was a learned vulnerability. If it all went to hell here, I couldn't shoot back or fly myself out of this one.

Flying on Pan Am Flight 001 I couldn't wait to get to Lebanon. Now I couldn't wait to get out of it. Happy to finally feel the plane was moving. We could leave troubled Beirut. Rumbling our way down the rough taxiway I couldn't wait to hear us power up and lift off. Felt a great sense of relief when we were cleared to the runway.

The sky was freedom. This day it would also be sanctuary. Often between points on the globe flying was a pleasant quiet time to just think. Nothing outside to see anyway at 30,000 feet. Travel then was a gift, a pleasure, not the drudgery it's become with narrow seats, inconsiderate, self-centered fellow travelers and small, difficult bags of bad peanuts.

All the seats on the early 707 were leather, big and roomy. The food service was on real china with real silverware. Dining choices were four to five stars. Steaks were freshly cooked and made to your order, liquor included. No extra fees or charges for anything. Stewardesses were stunning, friendly, and they pampered you.

Being airborne was in a sense asylum. It became a time when you could think and perhaps digest what you might have learned from the people in the last country you visited. A time to put things in perspective. Ingest and embrace whatever new meanings or understandings about the other people on this planet you just learned. All the while there was that other voyage happening on a level I still had not yet recognized.

Of course, there was no need for airport security or screening then. The airline staff was warm and welcoming, helpful, knowing the success of their airline depended on it. Still, it was more than a paycheck. There was pride and professionalism. So, staying on the plane wasn't uncomfortable.

A tall, slender, long-legged stewardess came by soon after departure from Beirut. She offered me a drink. She was attractive but looked like she could use a drink herself. Ever chivalrous, I offered her one of her own drinks. Maybe I wasn't entirely alone in my worry sitting down there on the tarmac. She said she hated this route. Beirut was always a dreaded stop over and the airline made the entire crew stay on the plane there.

We had added some new passengers at the airport. They melted into available seats, stiff, tense and alert. Seemed after a while they relaxed with the relief of successfully leaving that conflicted country.

Pretty sure my sense of fear was exacerbated by my time in combat. But you didn't need that experience to be troubled by heavily armed soldiers in close proximity.

India...

I believe Mumbai was mispronounced "Bombay" for well over a hundred years. This because the egocentric English during their expansionism in the mid–1800s simply couldn't pronounce it properly. Of course, they thought the indigenous people didn't pronounce it properly.

The main boulevard of Mumbai had beggars lined often three and four deep, vying for space, all with their hands out.

I had never seen this before anywhere I'd ever been. This heart-breaking visual was the case all the way from the airport to the hotel. At the five-star hotel, the ills and pain of the outside world were discharged, barred from entry. An early James Bond movie had convinced me to travel five-star. Custom tan, belt leather luggage, custom shirts, shoes and four-to-five-star accommodations. Expensive but blissful.

The huge two-story hand-carved doors in the lobby kept reality at bay.

Amazing to watch the citizens of this city, a mix of Buddhist, Hindu and Muslim going through the marketplaces downtown. All shopping together for food, water, and other of life's very same essentials. Equally essential to each of them. Yet their religions so diverse, a couple of belief systems even diametrically opposed. Striking that they all converged on universal themes yet were unwilling to admit or address their basic commonality.

The human need for religion has spawned so many separate and disparate beliefs.

My War with Vietnam

Each to our own embraced belief systems, we allow these accepted paradigms to govern our very lives. Our decisions, actions, non-actions.

Most on this planet have adopted one of the major monotheistic deity systems.

I will never. I lost any semblance of belief in the god myth in Vietnam. The old bromide, "There are no atheists in foxholes." Wrong. Exactly where and when it was I became a devout atheist was dropping infantry out of a helicopter onto a jungle battlefield.

Atheism isn't the absence of joy or contentment. It's the absence of delusion.

The acceptance that an explosion of evolution gave us reason. The great gift of this understanding is that we have just this one life, only a limited time to do good things, help others and hopefully spread goodwill and peace.

So, we better get about it daily and learn to love our lives and others, right now.

Likely amazing to any religious still reading but the non-religious can have as much goodwill toward others, hearts filled with love and compassion for all.

Being human requires high levels of compassion, deep reservoirs of understanding.

That's the magic truth my journey was showing me. I was staggering through the world alone but buoyed up by the unsolicited welcome warmth of others. It hadn't all sunk in yet, hadn't changed me that I could see or feel, but I was learning.

Other beings on this planet recognized me as another life form like themselves.

They then simply offered hope, succor, warmth, acceptance.

In Vietnam I watched the best and worst of human nature claw its way out of each of us daily. Human nature ... not the Devil with scaly skin and a bifurcated tail representing evil: the worst of our nature. And not God, the icon of our good side.

No cause and effect by omniscient forces or supernatural beings outside ourselves.

India...

Just pure, unadulterated human nature. All from within. Within each of us.

The innate savagery available to the human heart is staggering. The reservoir of moral justification for inhuman, inhumane acts on one another impressive and at once deeply, deeply troubling. Mystifying actually.

Illogical anyway that an omniscient being "Created us in his own image."

A perfectly great fabrication and construct for the archetype model; lambs need a shepherd. Perfectly great fabrication and construct for obeisance to a higher power.

But then, paradoxically, it puts us in a world where we each believe our theology, our concept of God and patronage to same is the right one. And all others wrong.

So, let the games and bloodshed begin.

Best dissection and explanation of the religious phenomenon is Dr. David Wilbur's book, *Power and Illusion: Religion and Human Need*. Likely on Amazon. Read it carefully. It's not a walk in the park.

What's really out there? On the other side? Seems a shame to think there's nothing at all doesn't it? Nothing going on after our death? After we shed these mortal coils?

Humans can't accept that. We as a species, as egocentric beings refuse to accept that this elaborate consciousness we think refined and so valuable just ends.

So, we conjure up the myth of life everlasting in heaven or hell. We share it with each other, cajole one another throughout our daily lives with this next destination, this mystical unknown experience. And without ever knowing the reality of it, on faith, like a dog with a tasty bone discovered in the park, we embrace it until we die.

But before we leave this life and do know what's next, we find ourselves commissioned, exhorted to perpetrate our beliefs on other people, other lands, other faiths and the next generation. If it weren't so absurd, diametrically opposed to reason and logic ... it would be comical. Sadly, it's not.

My War with Vietnam

As a rational human it's embarrassing. But so be it. We're all allowed, encouraged, forced to make our own choices.

We convince one another at churches, synagogues and mosques that this, here, today—isn't it. This life is only rewarded later in a five-star land beyond our ken as mere humans. But this is it! The great joy of life day by day, moment by moment, is life. Our lives.

To what purpose cries out the ever-stalwart logic?

Plato and Socrates believed our reward for a life well lived was, simply, a life well lived. We are animals, even as we believe of a higher order than cats, dogs and chimps. But are we that special? That different? Or is it arrogance that we are due more, owed more for our giant intellect?

Or is it simply fear?

We assume other species have no consciousness, are not truly self-aware, that they have no spirit or soul. We assume only we can ascend to a special afterlife.

The basic belief in an afterlife is an assumption taken on faith. It's based on millennia, eons of myths being retold over campfires even before the first written language. Told over and over by mere mortals like us who haven't yet been to the other side either. There must exist a finer place as our just deserts for the life well lived as believers until we died! No.

Can't believe that if I don't follow the rules and buy into one of the vended religions I'll end up roasting on the same spit as Hitler, Stalin or Pol Pot. Seems extreme for fudging on an expense report.

So go deep into your own jungle or dark forest where you keep your unassimilated thoughts, unproven ideas and fears. Start gardening there. Nurture thoughts, ideas and examine all misgivings. Prune when needed and kill all weeds.

Study and explore your own psyche until your beliefs are concise, unobscured, and cleared of the obtuse in your own reservoir of cogent thought. Dive in and swim through that lifetime of opinions and beliefs espoused by trusted others, those with an agenda and societal rants. If they stand the test of review by you ... for you, good for you. If not, keep questioning until answers are found.

India...

When in my career as a business and marketing consultant I would address a board meeting of a new client with this hypothesis: The worst reason for a business practice or protocol is "Well, we've always done it that way." ... Review and examine it with harsh objectivity. If it holds up to reason then carry on.

If it's obsolete, filled with fallacies or contradictions now, change it. And aren't you glad you reviewed it in time?

Australia...

Stayed in Sydney for a while in a great hotel. It was a tall, round, white building in an area known as King's Cross. First morning there in a cafe across the street an attractive waitress poured my coffee and asked me out for dinner and a play...

That night! While she filled my coffee cup! Just like that. Forward, aggressive.

Obviously, a blatant hussy. Mom had warned me about this woman. And I'd been looking for her ever since.

One thing led to another rather quickly. But I was surprised to discover afterwards, lying in bed together, I seemed to take more pleasure from holding her than I ever had before with anyone. Beyond the stirring in the loins something else was stirring. There was another need, another striving making its presence known.

We both knew I wasn't staying in Australia. It was just sex between two healthy humans satiating each other's needs. I don't remember being especially affectionate as a teenager before the war with girls after lovemaking.

I certainly wasn't with the prostitutes in the R&R cities the military checked for us. The Army doctors, worried as ever about our health, checked the girls for disease and issued cards. It was purely business with those girls. They were masters of both the act and the business and business was brisk.

Experience with women my first tour was limited to my imagination. Not many women ventured into the combat areas. A high

My War with Vietnam

point in the day of a helicopter pilot in our unit was a day off. They came rarely. And it didn't mean you didn't fly—you just didn't fly combat.

It meant a single ship, "Ass and Trash" mission. A euphemism for hauling people and cargo around the firebases. You would take ammo to a firebase or outpost, walking wounded from a medevac hospital to the bigger hospital at the main air base, guys on emergency leave and Donut Dollies.

As a morale builder the amazing Red Cross sent women to provide coffee, donuts and cheer to the troops. The Donut Dollies as they were dubbed also reminded us of what we were fighting for. Or at least why we were fighting to get back to America. They offered memories from home. They wore dresses and their legs were wonderful.

Everyone expects that when you're near a large idling helicopter there will be turbulence generated from the spinning main rotor blade. Not however if the pitch in the main blades are flat. Among all the things passed on from older combat pilots to new pilots was the nuance of putting a little pitch into the main blades if a Donut Dolly was anywhere near your idling aircraft. To watch them try unsuccessfully to hold down their skirts or dress against the turbulence and lift was a joy to see. Sigh.

It was during my second tour far away from the front lines as General Abrams' pilot I found myself doing the unexpected; telling a woman no. Refusing an offer of a dalliance for sexual pleasure from an attractive woman seemed odd for me, certainly out of character. But I did it twice. Men will tell each other, "Worst I ever had was great." And usually this was true. Being in Saigon meant being around admin offices and there were many. It takes a huge amount of logistical support to run a war.

Met a young woman, a sergeant in the Army who worked in supply. I took her to dinner one night at one of the amazing French restaurants in Saigon. We were both twenty years old, so it didn't take long to get to the discussion of addressing our physical needs. Mine were obvious. Hers were diabolical. She frankly told me she wanted to get pregnant by me. She had two or three more years to

Australia...

serve and wanted out. She felt she had made a mistake by joining and the fastest way a woman could be discharged from service was to become pregnant.

Having raised my younger brothers and sister while our single mom worked to support us, I knew I didn't want kids. The young woman had a plan though. She would get pregnant, get thrown out of the Army then have an abortion. I didn't want any part of that. And should she decide to keep the baby I also didn't want a kid growing up not knowing who their father was. So, I said no.

The second time I told a woman no was even more complicated. Officer's Calls are mandatory meetings in the military. Sometimes they are important. Some are just social. It was at one of these functions in Saigon, now Ho Chi Minh City, where I met, let's call her Molly. She was a lieutenant and a trauma nurse. She served at the other end of our medevac missions witnessing the most horrible wounds from screaming, crying, often dying soldiers.

She was statuesque and very attractive. I didn't notice at first that she never smiled. My mind was focused elsewhere. After a couple drinks she suggested we go to her place. She had a small apartment in a military housing building. Her room was bland and dull except for the starched and perfectly ironed military fatigue blouse hanging on the wall. The blouse had four black stars on each shoulder and the name Westmoreland over the pocket. I'm sure General Westmoreland hadn't been there and certainly wouldn't leave his shirt behind if he had. Just an attempt at a little humor.

As we had another drink the mood seemed serious, almost businesslike. She was on a mission. Abruptly she said, "Let's go to bed." With no apparent joy or interest, she took off her clothes, as did I.

The next while we were consumed with each other in pure animal lust. Lust and satiating needs is always good. But something wasn't right, didn't feel right. When our needs were met, she simply said, "Thanks. I got what I needed. There's a taxi on the corner that will take you back to your accommodations. Don't promise me anything. Don't call. Just leave."

Unable to muster a cogent response anyway, I got dressed and

My War with Vietnam

left not knowing what else to do or say. I never called her of course and it took me a while to figure out what had happened. I saw her once more at another Officer's Call.

Eye contact with her was suggestive enough that I realized another quickie could happen. I chose rather to walk away signaling a no, not interested. I felt the woman had apparently been drained of all compassion and warmth. No life left in her just getting through the day meeting her body's most basic needs. Not her fault perhaps through her job of sewing up soldiers, amputating their limbs or declaring them dead.

She had become cynical about life and perhaps men in general. I, through the same war, had become a different person and still didn't know what I didn't know. But I knew I didn't want to be intimate with this woman again in an empty, soulless tryst. I think even then I was beginning to recognize a need for more. Later, after the war I seemed to need the human touch a lot, even reaching out for it when I could.

Stayed in Australia longer than I planned. Actually, planning hadn't yet occurred to me. I seem to be floating along, carried forward in a current on a stream of living, of life. Meeting people, seeing new countries and experiencing life after war. When troubled again or satiated or when curiosity drove me I would go to the airport and get on Pan Am Flight One again. Off to another culture, accepted there and embraced by the warmth of humanity.

Maybe there wasn't any outward manifestation of the turmoil inside me. I was still, I believed, the monster I had become.

But maybe only I saw the monster, the non-human I had to be to get through war. Outwardly, maybe my visage was still the young man who, with what I was told, had a nice smile.

The curator of the Sydney Zoo then kept albino animals in his front yard across the bay from the Opera House. Pure white kangaroos, wombats, koalas all free to roam the manicured green lawn right down to the waterfront. I'm sure they're gone now. Likely politically incorrect now to keep only white animals in his yard.

Aussies are warm friendly people. It's one of the places on my travels I felt completely at home. I felt I could immigrate and prosper.

Australia...

But at least then you couldn't immigrate to this country unless they needed your skill or trade.

Imagine telling people you can't stay in their country unless you can contribute to their society? What gall! How politically incorrect can one be? Pilots were stacked up like cordwood after the war so I couldn't get a flying job there or stateside.

Italy...

Hailed a cab at the airport, which turned out to be a dingy, really "seasoned" Fiat. Wanted to see a little of Rome of course on the way to the hotel. And we're off.

The cabbie speaks English or really, "American" fairly well. There is a difference. Likely helps in his job.

Thought he would be bored having to do this for several tourists a day. Rather he seems to bubble over with enthusiasm pointing out ancient structures. Some even older than his Fiat...

The art, architecture and culture of this old city makes it one of the most amazing centers of civilization in the world. I'm a little tired from the flight, ready for my hotel, but he revels in his storytelling, and I'm caught up in it.

He looks over his shoulder often, making sure I see what he is pointing at and that I'm understanding his message. As we sliced our way around traffic I honestly began to believe we're going to die in a horrible collision. The thought of getting killed in a Rome traffic circle after leaving helicopter combat in Vietnam seems morbidly ironic. The cabbie is driving with one hand, gesticulating wildly with the other. Seems oblivious to our imminent death.

Don't remember when the cabbie turned off his meter. Seem to have a vague recollection but no acknowledgment on his part or mine that my sightseeing tour had now become his mission—not his fare. What is going on here with this gregarious man?

This had happened once before, in Sydney. I mentioned to the cab driver there taking me to my hotel he had a cool shirt and asked,

My War with Vietnam

"Where did you get it?" "Here, I'll show you mate." He turned off his meter, took me to his favorite men shop and parked the cab. Then he went in with me and helped me pick out a couple of shirts. Getting close to the hotel again he turned his meter back on.

I would always wonder throughout this journey if I was adopted or embraced so easily so often because I traveled alone. I almost never appeared at a cafe or restaurant with a built-in companionship, already encapsulated in a closed bubble of conversation.

Realizing how lucky I was to survive war at all, my aura might be changing. I was perhaps glowing with signals that said, "Thanks for letting me visit your country, you can't imagine the one I left. I'm lucky to be here." But maybe I appeared just lost or needy. Maybe I appeared to be a human obviously in need of repair. Perhaps everyone but me could see how I had such a tenuous hold on my own being.

This Italian cabbie makes his living from fares. Yet here he was taking time out of his day to openly display his pride in his city and country.

I remember I used to be proud of my country too. And it came to me just then, I wanted to be proud again. I wanted that back. That whole feeling of having a home had dissipated. I had become disconnected from my roots, my entire joyous childhood and growing up easy as an American. I'd been uprooted, set adrift and wasn't sure where I belonged anymore.

Where is home? What had changed? Where did my pride in America get lost?

I wasn't ashamed of how we acted as soldiers in Vietnam. There were atrocities—on both sides. But those incidents aside we acted with honor and fought hard.

We tried hard to win against both a fierce enemy and a myopic Washington, D.C.

I never saw or even heard about an act of cowardice on our side. Bravely fought.

But something had distanced me from my comfortable assumptions about my life and my country.

England...

Waited in line in a drizzly rain at a London theater to see "Midnight Cowboy." Theatrical film promotion wasn't the art and science it is now. All of us, Brits and me, thought we were going to watch an American Western.

Went to the Birmingham Small Arms factory outside London to buy a BSA motorcycle. Told the plant manager I wanted to learn about import/export perhaps as a business career. He said, "Well here's your first lesson, mate." He then had an engineer take my brand-new bike back out of its wooden crate, re-assemble it, and drove it around their track for six miles. Sold it to me used.

Saved me a bundle on export and import taxes.

He didn't have to do that. So why did he? Perhaps he was just connecting with another human being on the planet as best he could. Shared his wisdom with a complete stranger for no reason other than, I guess, what, humanity? Didn't cost him anything. Didn't net him anything but my gratitude. Higher education comes from the weirdest places.

Somewhere around the shored-up Dickens original bookshop a guy walking the opposite direction on the sidewalk on a London street says, "So how are things in the colonies, mate?"

Didn't want anything, just a great opening line. I guess I just looked American. Wasn't sure I wanted to though.

I wanted to blend in with every culture, mix in, disappear ... but couldn't. Apparently I was a marked man, an obvious American.

Couldn't ascertain the good or bad of this. But there was perhaps a currency then in being American.

At that time, we were still respected around the world as a nation.

In my office I look at the bookshelves and there is an eight-edition collection titled, "The History of the Decline and Fall of the Roman Empire" by Edward Gibbon. Wonder if should read at least the last volume again? When last I read it, I seem to remember that the empire fell apart because of the obvious corruption of their politicians. Its citizens had lost trust and faith in their leadership.

Looking at our republic today ... it just makes you wonder.

So many economic, political and foreign policy mistakes along with rampant corruption the last couple of decades we are no longer on a pedestal internationally.

We have even lost our self-respect. Witness the decisions we make about our politicians. With manipulated TV and social media pulverizing our consciousness, we are in danger of becoming just another banana republic. Shameful.

We should as a culture demand more than televised sound-bites and press-released answers to serious questions facing our country. We should demand actual thought-out solutions to our nation's ills. Not just easily available predigested crap. Not polished visual optics. We should get signed legal contracts on our politicians' positions. This, so they can't just say what they think is needed in front of different crowds, vacillating on important points sometimes from morning to afternoon.

If they get elected and change their position, violate their own campaign promises, they have broken a serious contract and are worthy of being impeached or fired.

We need leadership—not show business. Shame on us for settling. Shame on us for allowing politicians to hire hucksters who know and understand how to manipulate us and our thoughts. I worry about a nation that elects its politicians like we elected prom queens in high school. Who looks good with the football captain? None really ever vetted for integrity or leadership.

England...

Flight school and officer training took a year. I took a month off afterward in Southern California, then went to Vietnam. I still remember standing about halfway back in the plane waiting behind other soldiers to get off the Boeing 707 at the huge airbase outside Bien Hoa.

War was such an abstract to me. I remember thinking as I walked to the door to get off the plane that it would be pitch black outside. Even though I knew it was mid-day.

Flying in Vietnam was an education. I knew I was learning a lot about everything. Every day it seemed I'd learn something new, about me, life, and human nature. Learned things I never thought I'd know.

Photograph taken by a London street photographer (author's collection).

Learned things I didn't want to know. All of us did. We were all so young. We weren't just learning about life and death and the shearing, sudden, subtle difference between the two. We were young and learning good reasons for living.

We thought we had also embraced equally good ones for dying. Like not wanting to return home crippled for life with missing limbs. Or blind. Or with your nuts blown off like that one guy. Way too many of us went home in pieces. This, in spite of our sincere "Kill me if I'm wounded" pacts we all made, then violated with our copilots. On any terms it seems life was worth the pain.

My War with Vietnam

Just months in-country, insidious caustic doubts seeped into all your psychic wounds like an acid. Something about this war wasn't right. You couldn't prove it of course. Couldn't even really talk about it much. We were deliberately left out of the discussions and media assault by the military. We couldn't figure it out.

But we knew.

If the growing pains endured switching from patriot to cynic, childhood to manhood, fearful to fearless and back again weren't enough, there was the daily drug. It was a free drug with freaky, exhilarating highs and sea bottom lows.

Adrenalin. And something else too.

Something that worked you every bit as hard yet didn't have a name. It came with the rock and a hard place question; if this war is wrong, why do I feel so good? So vital? So important?

With time, looking back I can see through the dichotomy. It's natural enough to be excited about having your own nimble, powerful helicopter when you're only twenty. Taking that aircraft into the middle of a fire fight to save a soldier's life is an adrenaline explosion, a rewarding and life altering act.

For myself and hopefully whomever we picked up out of the fray.

Hearing an emergency radio call for a medevac, knowing you're close enough to answer that call is an incredible rush. You could pass on it. You could even pretend you didn't hear it. You're the Aircraft Commander. The other kids on your plane, your copilot, crew chief and door gunner can't call you on it.

But someone's wounded or otherwise in the real deep shit ... and they need you. The reason they're wounded is because right now they're taking fire. Infantry in a firefight or a downed air crew with the enemy closing in. Getting them out immediately to medical care means you're going to take fire going in after them.

Still, you go.

I was important beyond my years. There's a price though. And, it turns out, a deferred payment plan as well.

With time, some slow healing and distance, I can see I had developed a love-hate relationship with that war. I truly wished I'd

England...

never gone. And certainly, I wish I'd never seen some of the things I saw there.

Yet, I wouldn't trade the experience for anything.

When I see a teenager today all buzz haircut, baggy pants halfway down his ass, acne, tattoos and skateboards, I shiver. We couldn't have been thrown into that hellish nightmare when we were really that young could we? Aside from Robert McNamara who at a late date decided to either clear the air or purge his conscience with his book, what were the rest of the politicians, leaders and self-proclaimed statesman thinking of?

Really, we were still just children.

Scotland...

Unlike America, if you are by yourself anywhere in Europe at a pub or café you won't get a table to yourself. You might if it's slow. But, as mealtime approaches, as the crowd increases, if another single comes in, the host or maître de introduces you to someone you have never met. And you share your table with a wonderful stranger, perhaps even a brand-new friend.

Americans are incredibly territorial. Test it. You step on an elevator in America, it's your territory. One other person comes on at another floor and you divide the elevator floor space exactly in half. Another comes on and you all move, dividing the elevator floor into thirds. Not an indictment—just an observation.

Other countries people stand closer. Here we would take offense.

Scotland was an entire country of new friends. Felt very much at home there. Could even be home. After all, my Dad was adopted. Who knew his background, his ancestry? He and his brother were both left on the porch of an orphanage in Maine. Mom's side was French-Canadian from Newfoundland.

I'm told I'm one-eighth Mic Mac, a Native American tribe in Maine where I was born. Not at all sure what the fraction means.

After getting past the thick but lyrical accents I discovered a slew of new folks trying to understand me and the war. They helped me. That wasn't their goal of course. But it came about, developed as they kept trying to get to know me.

They all kept asking questions, kept drilling deeper...

My War with Vietnam

Didn't know it yet but they, trying to understand me, helped me. I was getting closer to the old me. Somewhere inside me still was the kid who didn't think he had an enemy in the world ... and didn't until sent to war.

Greece...

Spent a week there, much more I think. Wonderfully warm people and culture.

Dancing and Ouzo.... Their outlook on life glowed like smiles above their heads. Don't these people ever stop dancing and drinking?

Even the chubby, swarthy waiter at an outdoor café seemed to lightly dance, float and hum as he went from table to table. Content and happy... I'm envious.

How do I get back there from where I am now?

I know I'm not happy anymore. Some things came to me quickly on this journey. Good example: discovering I wasn't happy. Other things took longer to perceive and understand like broken bones do to heal. Looking for reasons to smile or think wonderful thoughts wasn't an effort before. Now it's a laborious task.

The obvious wasn't obvious any longer.

The most natural endearing sights; two people walking on a beach, talking or not, but holding hands, children laughing playing catch, puppies chasing each other ... were blocked. Nothing broke through the boundaries of perception I'd put up. Nothing got in. Nothing could get to me.

I wouldn't allow it. I was protecting myself from a disorder, war. That it didn't exist for me any longer made no difference yet. But just now there's a void, an empty space where happiness and contentment used to live. Could be it's chewed up or crushed forever. Or maybe just lurking around a hidden revelation or epiphany, playing hide and seek with me. I wonder if I can find that again. They were embedded in me before, taken for granted from birth in America. I grew up with them.

In Greece I stayed in a pure white village, can't remember the name, overlooking an azure sea. The old village was built like Swallows build nests in caves and under bridges. Little homes had common walls, almost communal. The boutique hotel I stayed in was built the same, separated only by a cobblestone walkway and dirt path, from buildings on either side.

I'll never know what the villagers saw in my eyes. Could they see I needed healing? Did they know I needed to be re-embraced as a human and welcomed back into the fold? Was it obvious I needed to be told, "All is well. Everything is going to be okay again. You're going to be okay."

And if my need was so obvious, so visible, why did they feel they should help?

Why bother? Do not know why for sure. Suspect they just reached out to a stray needing some attention. Whatever the reason, they did reach for me.

Not sure what perhaps frightening visage they saw in me. But what I saw in their eyes was acceptance and welcome. I had changed so much I felt the monster.

Unseemly things had been growing inside me and festering for a long time.

Belief and value systems had become corrupt with the bankruptcy of human kindness. I didn't know how or even yet that I needed to reach out for help. Didn't need to reach though.

I was bereft of feelings. Overdrawn on trust and understanding as currency. But strangers kept making donations and deposits into my account.

The innate kindness in people everywhere shone like beacons. If I were a ship at sea on a stormy night I'd see lighthouses. They were everywhere.

Total strangers asked, "How are you?" Then waited patiently for my answer.

Greece...

I was beginning to slowly understand. Something was happening on a level I wasn't privy to yet. But I began to recognize I had stopped feeling anything. Anything at all. I was numb.

It was likely a subconscious choice for my survival. Don't remember exploring it, debating with myself, "Should I or shouldn't I go comatose for the rest of this war?"

Becoming numb had likely saved my sanity while at war. I don't see how anyone can witness carnage on any scale and not shut down their perception sensors. It would be a data overload of dangerous proportions.

First few days watching other aircrews get shot down or young soldiers get killed you were horrified. But you couldn't stay in that altered state. Dangerous to linger there. You had to get past that so you could operate successfully in that environment.

Don't remember when I stopped being horrified at the carnage around me. But quite sure I stopped feeling anything at all that same day. Stop feeling. And go to a dark place in your heart for the rest of your tour just to get through it.

But everywhere I went on this globe afterward total strangers tried to make me understand I couldn't stay there. Shouldn't. I didn't need to be numb anymore.

As a matter of fact, staying numb would deny me the full privileges and benefits of being human. This was true almost everywhere I traveled.

Not far from my hotel I could see into the courtyard of a small tidy home. For the time I was there a ritual formed. I anticipated it, waited and watched for it like a predator, a raptor on high from my hotel balcony. Dinner time, late evening, the day cooling. A family of five would sit at the table in their courtyard to eat.

Mom, Dad and three children just eating together.

Too far to hear and lip reading was out but I imagined, "What did you learn in school today?" "How did work go today dear?" "How did tryouts go today for soccer?" Family questions. Caring questions. Home questions.

France...

Felt tolerated in Paris, not really welcome. The French allowed me to eat in their restaurants and bistros, drink their fine wines, and allowed me to enjoy their landmarks and scenery. But I was ignored. Not forcibly or verbally ostracized, just ignored. The sooner I left their country the better was the only thing we seemed to agree on.

On the flight out of Paris I met an Army Special Forces Sergeant. He was going home after his second tour in Vietnam. When I got on the plane, in spite of his full-dress uniform with four rows of battle ribbons on his chest it seemed no one else saw him. Or maybe didn't want to see him.

Didn't want to engage in a conversation. Could be, like a lot of folks, they might not want to hear what he had to say. People kept moving past him without looking at the empty seat next to him. So, I sat there.

He had been wounded at the Battle of Kham Duc. That short fight was the most ferocious and intense combat the Vietnam War ever saw. It was also one of America's worst losses. Masses of North Vietnamese soldiers overran a small American Special Forces outpost. With close quarter fighting and hand to hand combat, 259 American and South Vietnamese soldiers were killed, hundreds more wounded. Thirty-one American soldiers were deemed Missing in Action in only the first 24 hours. Eight aircraft were shot down trying to help the guys on the ground.

All this carnage in two days, just 48 hours.

The wounds he had from Kham Duc were serious enough he

My War with Vietnam

needed nearly a year to recover. Probably could have been medically discharged but insisted on staying in. Then he insisted on another tour. Wanted to go back and fight. That's Special Forces for you.

He was quiet at first in his own world, his own pain. Respectful when we introduced ourselves, then quiet again. By the time Pan Am Flight One was on its leg out of Paris he had been in eleven countries. I asked him when he left Saigon.

His cryptic response was, "Couple days ago."

Then I was quiet. I had been stopping often, learning, discovering along the way. And the hard, dark shadows at the edge of my being were gently being chipped away by complete strangers I met everywhere. I never asked them to help.

Inherently, no matter the color of their skin the human race just needs and wants the same things, acceptance. Understanding. Love. And the natural instinct is to show and offer those traits before receiving them.

He wasn't going to let anyone show him anything until he had dragged all his baggage and horror back home. He would deal with it there when he finally figured it out.

Had to say something so I said, "You gotta get off the plane."

The statement startled him, brought him back to the present with me.

He said, "What?" I said, "You gotta get off this plane. Next stop. Promise me, okay?" "For what? I just want to get home."

"I know. So do I. But you can't just jump out of hell, leave that environment abruptly and carry all the pain home with you. We've been in a place no one should ever have to go. It's an enormous chasm away from where we should be now."

"Not sure what you mean," he said.

"Not sure myself yet," I responded slowly. "But I'm starting to understand some things. Look, there's a bunch of people, all strangers in fact, out there in nearly every country we land in that would like to show you and me the way back. I didn't get it at first. But these strangers have reached out to pull me back from the edge almost everywhere I stopped."

France...

Funny but until I voiced this to him, I hadn't seen my own journey with such clarity. We have bridges to build and cross throughout life. Coming back from a war to life as we envisioned it before wouldn't be easy without help.

"Way back to what?" he wanted to know.

"Normal life? Real life, I think. Life in America? Home? Not sure but no one should have to go where we were, where we've been. Now we have to get back to life without killing and the danger of dying if we don't kill. No one wins a war, everyone loses. But if you've been in a war, you lose more than the rest. You and I aren't who we think we are anymore. Not who we were anyway. And we have a long ways to go. I only just learned that from others on this planet."

The stewardess stopped at our aisle first and said to him, "What do you need soldier, I'm buying." It brought a tiny smile to his face since he knew the drinks were free. We both recognized that she had passed everyone else to serve him first. Maybe to honor his service sprawled like a colorful garden of battle ribbons and medals across his chest. Maybe he wasn't as far gone as I was. Maybe he was tougher than me. Still, talking to him helped me in a weird way.

"And listen, when you get home and things aren't what they seem, don't quit on us, the rest of us. Don't give up. If you start to wonder where humanity is, buy as many Billie Holiday records as you can find and listen to her. Then reach out to the rest of us. We're there for you. ... But you gotta get off the plane, man."

Ireland...

Why is it every culture figures out a local vegetable or plant to distill and ferment to create booze? Who thought of it first? Had to be an accident the first time. Fallen fruit under a tree turns. Some caveman smells it, thinks it smells good and dares Neanderthal Ned to try eating it. Ned then gets shitfaced but happy and funny, finally showing some personality.

And the word spreads. Potatoes become vodka in Russia. Cactus is Mexico's answer to sobriety. Somewhere in history as humans spread throughout the world this phenomenon caught on.

I remember one early morning leaving a pub in Belfast. It was raining and I wasn't prepared. Should have been. Knew it was looking like rain when I left the hotel. Come to think of it, it looked like rain the entire time I was there. But no umbrella or other rain gear, nothing.

A stranger walking by saw my dilemma. So, he, on a whim, from some well of kindness or humanity inside him, offered to share his umbrella to his next stop. As luck would have it, another local pub. We walked together nearly arm in arm sharing his tiny shelter from the rain.

Arriving at another warm, inviting tavern up the street I was introduced to the gathering there. For the next while in that wonderful happy building, I couldn't buy my own drinks.

I learned two important things there that night.

First, the intricacies of mixing real Irish Coffee. Properly done,

My War with Vietnam

more complicated than you might imagine. Spoon held just under the surface of the coffee pouring rich, real cream into the spoon just as it breaks the surface, so it spreads beautifully into a thick layer over strong coffee and excellent Irish whiskey at the bottom.

After one of those artful creations though, I switched drinks. Went back to the aged, single-malt Scotch I had discovered in Scotland.

More importantly, I also embraced that humans everywhere feared and at once cherished all the same things. Doesn't matter if you live in a penthouse overlooking the Thames or a grass hut barely clearing the mangroves in a Sumatran swamp.

I was to be reacquainted with the basic concept of being a human all over the world. Kept relearning it anew every stop around the world. I was being reintroduced to humanity from the ash covered, inhuman landscape of war by my fellow humans. I was handheld, comforted and counseled by total strangers everywhere I went.

Most didn't know perhaps they were helping me at all. But their kindness, their warmth, their welcoming me to their country and often their homes and families was cathartic. They couldn't know the reparations they were enabling in me.

But I was starting to feel things again ... strange that I had forgot or disabled lifelong certitudes to get through the chaos.

No one hated me and I hated no one. I had friends everywhere I went.

And only had enemies in one small but beautiful country in Southeast Asia by political mandate.

Spain...

There are no real language barriers. People can communicate if they wish: sign language, pointing at objects, yelling. Actually though, repeating yourself louder and louder doesn't really help.

Met a family on a Spanish beach who just swept me up into their life for a couple of days. They were from Portugal over on holiday. The little tribe's mother was the real outgoing one. She epitomized the title "Matriarch."

Everyone deferred to her will or instructions, including me. She would order food at restaurants for her husband and two kids. With a look at me she would also order for me, which was helpful, delightful actually. Not even uncomfortable since I couldn't read the menu at the non-tourist cafes she picked anyway.

Then she would decide for everyone it was time to take a walk on the beach but too early to go in the water. She was heavy set. No. She was fat. And given so easily to the human magic of touching and smiling and hugging and laughing. What a life force so filled with compassion and kindness.

What a tremendous gift this woman was to all of mankind.

And especially, just then, to me. I'm sure her life was filled with responses in kind everywhere she went from everyone she ever met in her life. Hope so. Don't remember her name, just her touch.

She taught me how to hug, really. It isn't a grip on your shoulders or patting your back. The word describing a hug best is engulfing. Arms overlapping in back, heads bowed, side-by-side, ear-to-ear, touching one another. Can't get closer to another fully dressed. The proper hug isn't over until that person knows they are safe or loved or cherished or have been truly missed.

She basically adopted me, treating me as a child of hers for the time we spent together. Of all the things I was beginning to miss about America, family was topping the list. I knew they would accept me as is, no matter what. No matter what I'd become.

They had to, right? That's what family is for, what it's about. I had traveled so far away from who I was, who they thought I was, they might not know me anymore. Still, I felt the need to decompress. More time, meet more people, see new countries. Or maybe just resolve some things before I saw family again.

Or maybe get closer to me again before I foisted myself on my family.

I was alienated from me, from who I thought I was or should be.

It was an uncomfortable realization.

Africa...

Got into a pickup football game on a lake's beach outside Johannesburg. Watched for a while on what were apparently the sidelines. Teams became uneven and one of the players simply waved me over. We drew plays in the sand with our fingers. Pointing at me meant I was to run this line in the sand. Just like home, America, full speed, break-neck full-tackle, shirts versus skins to designate teams.

Began to feel homesick. Maybe for a younger time and a better place. But they were both gone. I can't go there again, ever. And I'm not ready to go home yet anyway.

I had played well enough in college to get asked to try out for the Coca Cola semi-pro football team. The offer wasn't based on scholastic play but rather our amazing and highly organized sandlot games played at city parks all around Pasadena. Between dirt bikes in the California desert, football and helicopters it's amazing I even survived my own youth.

I weighed the football offer against a friend who had an apartment in Hawaii with an extra room. Stay in Los Angeles and get the crap kicked out of me as the quickest but smallest guy to ever play semi-pro football ... or go to Hawaii and surf ... hmmm?

I believe it was that first five-hour flight across the Pacific realizing how far I had to travel to get to Hawaii where I was first bitten by the travel bug. What a planet.

Pakistan...

Everyone in Karachi seems angry. Or is it me? Maybe this is a reflection of my own anger. Anger was the common emotion in combat. Fear went away soon after flying into combat. Replaced by an acceptance of your likely death approaching an LZ to pick up grunts. Replaced as well by adrenalin.

No. It's not me. Karachi is crowded, hot, unattractive, with limited choices for food or drink. There is an acknowledgment, a begrudging acceptance apparently that this is life as good as it gets with few ways to improve it. There's nothing really but desert outside the city limits where all the little streets defer to one road.

I'm uncomfortable here. These people are uncomfortable judging by the unguarded looks of disdain I see and feel.

I grew and learned on my travels becoming closer to me and perhaps purging some demons. I've learned in the years since that my journey was only to begin a lifelong quest of finding myself. Just like everyone does. Bit of a side trip not everyone takes with the war perhaps. But all of us search, learn and grow.

The excitement and most of the pain is gone now. There are memories to deal with though. Still and for always, I guess.

Persia...

I know. But the many people I've met from Iran, always say Persia when asked where they are from. Stopped briefly in Tehran. One of the few places where I didn't feel entirely welcome or at home. Set out to explore anyway.

Cab took me down a few winding, tree-lined streets until we hit a roadblock. Not military, just a party that had spilled into the streets. Thought at first it was a masquerade ball. The beautiful traditional costumes indicated to my cabbie we had bumped into a wedding party.

If this was only one wedding it must be for a king and queen. Maybe he was wrong. It looked more like a coronation or other affair of state. All these people couldn't possibly be related to the bride or groom. The now suburb of Tehran, really only a neighborhood within the growing urban sprawl, had once been a separate village. It had lost its name but hadn't lost its identity.

Likely there were people old enough to remember the village as it was. Likely the elders never left home when Tehran showed up at their door and engulfed them.

Several countries I visited it was not uncommon to find people who had grown up, married, lived and would die within a few blocks of where they were born.

In spite of my welcomes almost everywhere this alone kept me feeling like the outsider. Here I was traveling the globe stopping to look at windows of culture like displays in a mall.

My War with Vietnam

The entire neighborhood for blocks around was celebrating this pairing of families. Such rich pageantry and ceremony for a joining. The bride and groom seemed to glow. The adulation of the crowd fed on it. If happiness is an energy this crowd was going nuclear.

Children not yet old enough to even understand marriage were caught up in the celebration and ceremony. The happiness of their moms and dads and the whole crowd made them smile and laugh. All hoped for this union to be blessed, filled with contentment and safety for the bride and groom for the rest of their lives.

Found myself consciously wishing the same for them. They didn't even know who I was sitting there in the back of a cab watching. But I wanted the best for them.

I hadn't ignored people's messages to me around the world. Never turned away from a handshake or failed to return a smile. But those reactions came easily and at first were only automatic, robotic. There was no internal reaction from me.

Eventually though, at some point the human race wore me down to a fresh start. People began to restore my faith in us. They kept trying to welcome me back through so many countries. I began to re-embrace being human. With this wedding party spilling over into a dusty street I think I was starting to reach out or reach back to other humans.

When you have a cold or the flu it's difficult to say when you are starting to get better. You might be in agonizing discomfort for a few days. But the exact moment you started to heal and feel better is lost, hard to identify. Not sure this wedding was my turn around at all. Just remember feeling something again, for someone else.

Kept traveling and visiting with humans all over the world. Invited into homes, discussions, dinners, American movies with subtitles and catharsis. To a degree I purged some demons along the way. Nearly all I met wanted to know what was really going on in Vietnam. After two tours I still wasn't sure. It would be a couple decades before I was.

Iceland...

CRAP. Neal, the stringer, the war correspondent and devout cynic is coming down the aisle as we board in Heathrow for Iceland. Doesn't ask, just plops down in the empty seat next to me and says, "Hey, last leg Army. Finally going home?"

"Almost. I'm getting off in Reykjavik for a while. Been learning my way around the world." I thought for a moment and said, "Hey, hope you're not headed for another conflict, like in America?"

"Nope, going to go home to Chicago and marry my girl. Going to go to work for the local paper and settle down, make babies. Three she tells me. And write about politics. As if that will ever be interesting."

"You should be happy ... excited. You don't sound enthusiastic about it."

"I'm not thrilled about day to day at a newspaper. This life of mine is an adrenaline rush and highly addictive. But if I don't stop my whirlwind tour of strife and grief the girl won't marry me. And I am enthusiastic about her."

"Sounds like she's a smart one," I offered. "I hope she makes you happy."

"Thanks Army."

We're both quiet for a moment listening to an announcement from the cabin crew. "You're wrong, Neal. You know, about everything you told me before.... Life isn't about fighting. It's all about caring and hope."

My War with Vietnam

"Hope? Maybe, maybe. We'll see. This woman is my hope. My last I think. I've been immersed in the world's killing and dying for ten years now. She's never even seen anyone die violently. Never watched another human hate so fiercely that they killed someone else ten feet away. I'm going to soak up her innocence, draw somehow from her purity and try to get back to whoever or whatever it was I used to be. Like to see if I can still be who I was before I learned to reach for a camera instead of helping or trying to stop what's about to happen."

"Long journey there and back. Hope it works out for you. I mean that."

I was wrong. About language, communicating. In Reykjavik I learned there are indeed language barriers. Icelandic has no root words you can identify. I don't think they even understand each other when you listen to their conversations.

I think they're faking it, making up noises and language as they go to impress the tourists. It's that unique. The surprise came when I found they were taught better English than I in their public schools.

The city of Reykjavik makes you feel like you haven't left Europe yet. Quaint, spotlessly clean, most of it old village style buildings like in Frankfurt and Brussels. Outside their one city is a land filled with geologic wonders. Geysers, streams hot enough to give off steam yet meandering through green grasslands.

It's also filled with a people truly misnamed "Icelanders" Their warmth as a people bubbles right up to the surface like the lava in their volcanoes. They should all be wearing signs around their necks, "Welcome to our country ... we know we've got a good thing going here."

Amazed to learn that women there have had equal rights in property and voting for nearly eight hundred years. The first parliament on the planet was formed there. No wonder everyone I met was so obviously proud of their country. Reminded me of a cabbie I met in Italy once.

Home...

Oddly, the coming home didn't work out too well. Today if someone finds out you were military they thank you for your service. Well intentioned and appreciated, of course. But the most powerful thing to say to a Vietnam veteran is, "Welcome home." We didn't hear that for our first three to four decades back.

Fears don't leave just because you leave Vietnam or any other theater of war I suspect. They take a while to go away. Some never do.

Vietnam was like being kept in a dark room. No windows, no doors, no light anywhere. I had been in a state of terror and exhaustion for a year and a half. Suddenly, one October morning I was set free. I stepped back into brilliant sunshine and complete personal freedom. Mind and body intact. The mornings after I came home were decidedly different from Vietnam's black uncertainty.

Once stateside, certainty returned to focus, and it was followed instantly by undiluted joy and elation.

I wanted to exercise my mind. I wanted to learn all I could, read everything. I wanted to talk with the intellectuals, tell them what I knew of the world, of people. And mostly, of the awesome things I had learned about myself.

I wanted to run faster and jump higher than any human ever had. I wanted to throw myself down soft green hills, roll to the bottom, land on my feet and run forever as I did as a child. I felt I could play every instrument in the orchestra like a virtuoso and win every athletic event I could enter. Yes, I wanted to show off a little.

My War with Vietnam

For being alive! Not for a crowd or the girl next door. For me.

Now, when I think of those who would never come home, I feel selfish for having reveled in my good fortune. But that didn't quash my spirits then. I had made it!

I was really alive. And that had never meant quite so much to me before.

There were other emotions, feelings and sensations to deal with though. All part of the "psychological adjustment" to peacetime civilian life. Sometimes I felt revulsion at what I had seen and taken part in. Guilt over willingly going to a war that I then didn't understand disturbed me a lot at times. I could not rationalize my guilt away. Eventually though, I have come to believe, I was far less culpable than the elected officials responsible for that travesty.

Yet, this is next to no consolation at all. It still bothers me.

I was often deeply troubled by and again, felt surprisingly guilty, over the lottery of fate that decided, I should live, and others should die. What serendipitous force determined that a man sitting next to me in the cockpit of an aircraft, with a wife and three children at home should die and I should not? If there is reason and logic not just names pulled out of some celestial hat behind "that" force, I hope I fulfill whatever purpose it is that made my survival possible.

* * *

I've been back from Vietnam for fifty years.

In the beginning, fears, rather than memories, were my strongest and most frequent sensation. Fears come in all sizes. Some are large and can fill me nearly to overflowing. If not kept under control, these large sudden fears manifest themselves as panic or shock.

A fear of this size consumed me for an instant on an early, quiet Los Angeles morning. Having experienced several weeks of peace after returning from Vietnam, unneeded defenses were slowly being worn down. Suddenly, there was an explosion and for a split second I was reliving the terror of my first night-time rocket attack at Cu Chi. I was actually relieved to discover that Los Angeles was experiencing a major earthquake.

Home...

There are also small, gnawing fears. These fears must periodically be dealt with or somehow suppressed. One fear I get, now as I grow older, is having to go back to another war somewhere. With all the flight training I received, I was told that I would be called before an untrained man on the street would be.

Age has its rewards after all. They won't take me now.

Sometimes these fears and memories trigger larger, more terrible concerns. I worry that this nation's leaders, willingly, for suspect motives, sacrificed 58,715 American lives and untold thousands of Vietnamese lives on a stalling action.

They knowingly merely postponed what those in power knew to be inevitable.

The fear of personally going back to war lessens with age. But, the concern and the shame I have for our buck-passers and flesh-pressers, simply grows with perspective and time. This claim is not unfounded.

There are even smaller, but no less demanding fears. Some take a great deal of time to show up. Sometimes we live with fears, adjusting to them without realizing what they are. I discovered this for myself not long ago.

A few years after Vietnam, I "looked" for an old friend from Flight School. I have been in his town. His last name is listed in the phone book. I didn't call. I have been to the small airport where he used to work and failed to ask if anyone knew him. Another friend who travels between my city and that of my flight school comrade has offered to look him up for me. I have stalled for so long this offer is no longer made.

If I choose, I have the means to contact his family. I haven't. I won't. After a year of intense flight training and fun, Ron and I lost track of one another in Vietnam. Since I heard he had drawn decent duty, his chances of returning home were very good. Upon leaving Vietnam, however, I ran into another classmate who said that we lost over forty percent of our Flight School graduating class in combat. Maybe Ron wasn't one of these.

I don't know. I never will know.

My War with Vietnam

Ron had raised loving life to an art form. He was gregarious, nearly bohemian in lifestyle. He had studied acting before getting into the Army and seemed to have the right quip or quote for any occasion, complete with appropriate histrionics.

Ron was brighter than most of our instructors and delighted in helping them illustrate that fact.

It was his idea, the time as Officer Candidates that the entire company showed up at morning formation with our bright orange "solo flight badges" buttoned over the wrong pocket. This gross deviation from dress uniform would have gone unnoticed in spite of our fifty barely suppressed smiles, had it not been for one late arrival who had not heard the word.

Naturally, this oddball made us stick out like fifty sore thumbs.

Still, we enjoyed the prank and camaraderie even throughout the punishing push-ups. Later, the mere mention of the training officer's expression as he saw through our little plot sent us into spasms of hysterical laughter.

Ron made military life bearable and military discipline laughable. Even the butt of much well-timed humor. He was fun loving and life was precious to him. That's how I remember him. And I'm going to always imagine him living life to the fullest. I dropped any pretense of my search long ago. I know this is a form of denial. But I'd rather believe him to be alive yet never see him again, than to discover his beautiful life was wasted in that stupid goddamned war.

Strangely, the war sometimes seems like it happened just yesterday.

Occasionally I found myself writing this book about it in the present tense.

Sometimes, still awash in remembrances, I feel like I just stepped down off the toe of a Huey skid.

Still, I've accomplished much since then. I've done well, done badly and grown through the pain. I've many times declared myself healed. I know I mostly am healed, healthy, and happy. That war shouldn't be a problem or even much of an issue at this late date.

So, how is it that a simple human gesture could bring me to my

Home...

Years later, still troubled (photo by Pat Crist, author's collection).

emotional knees?

My youngest brother was getting married at an elegant and sweet little ceremony in the backyard of a friend's home. It was warm and sunny. Southern California was doing its best for all of us. The old ritual complete, there were cousins and aunts galore to mingle with. It was fun.

As I was just about the last to leave, I saw one of my cousins moving right toward me. Craig is the usually jovial, good humored one. But he looked different somehow. He stopped in front of me and held out his hand to shake mine, then held it. I could feel he needed to say something important. Maybe even tough or uncomfortable for him.

He simply said, "I don't know if anyone ever told you this. Maybe no one has ever said it before. I just wanted to thank you for what you did in Vietnam. I appreciate what you did and what it must have cost you. I'm sorry I never said it before. Thank you."

My War with Vietnam

If I'm truly healed, and it's really all behind me, it should have been easy to just say something flip like, "Thanks Craig. That was nice." I probably did as a defense mechanism. But, if I'm truly healed, how is it that a simple human gesture like Craig's could have the effect it did on me?

I don't know for sure what I said. I do know it took every strength I had to get to my car before I started crying. It wasn't just a manly little weep. It was decades of pent-up pain, frustration, fears and remorse at my loss of innocence, my loss of trust in our system, my loss of friends I should still have and my remorse for going there. And, I think, probably so much more I still don't comprehend.

No one ever had thanked me before. I didn't believe I needed it. I couldn't believe either, that the simple gesture could pull me back down-so-far so quickly. It obviously is not something I've left too far behind.

But I don't want to wear that war with my heart on my shirt-sleeve.

It's funny what we think we need and don't need. Animals are so good at determining exactly what they need. They seldom ever try to get more than they need, or anything they don't need at all. The human race however, self-proclaimed superiors of these lowly beasts, has drugs, alcohol, unhealthy relationships with one another, wars, child abuse, and more.

You'd think, with intellect, our only pure separation from the animals, we would be better at determining our "needs." I certainly wish I were. We're a strange lot.

I'm back in Southern California. I still love burgers, football, the beach and girls.

I call them women now. My friends tell me there's still a lot of little boy left in me. This is okay. I'm surprised though. I think they mean I still have a sense of curiosity about how and why human nature works. I can still be surprised ... and disappointed.

I'm still amazed at what we fight over. It's always property or ideologies.

We should fight against poverty, illiteracy or disease as hard.

Home...

It seems the human sentiment strong enough to start wars is, "I'm right—you're wrong!" or "That's mine!"

I'm not qualified to preach, just observe, as a man who experienced a war.

And my observations lead me to believe we should be better than that as a species. Above it.

But if we can't stop wars, I know without question we shouldn't send teenagers to fight them. Teenagers should be left home to discover life, careers, sports, and rediscover sex every weekend. True love every month. They shouldn't be catapulted unprepared through a baptism of fire and blood then bungee-corded back to America. Unprepared again. And so many don't even come home.

Children ... born, fed, reared, loved, educated, cared for by parents and loved ones for eighteen years then killed by political mandate. This is the only lasting truth and essence of any war ever fought in any country at any time throughout history.

When I got back I was just over twenty-one years old. Yet I had aged spiritually too much to fit in. I know I returned world weary, out of step with my peers. Too old for my age. The things I had learned and experienced had no real application in normal life. Two and a half years of credits that didn't apply toward graduation.

Looking much like a fugitive, I've dodged nearly all of society's conventions and institutions.

Most of my friends married late in college. To their individual joy and torment, they have produced children. Their children's children are older now than I was when I went to Viet Nam. I see our young today and I can't believe anyone could send an eighteen-year-old to war.

They're smarter, better educated today. But somehow more fragile, even less sure of themselves than we were. While they probably need not worry about a nuclear holocaust, we've given them lesser but so many more uncertainties to grow up with. I still have no children and have never married.

My core of early friends all have careers they have diligently and energetically pursued to varying degrees of success. I have as eagerly

My War with Vietnam

jumped from position to position, new challenge to new challenge. Usually, I have been my own boss.

Apparently I'm unwilling to leave my fate to the decisions of others. This is a scary lesson I know I learned in Vietnam.

I have been a long-haul truck driver, professional pilot, copywriter, law student, account executive for advertising agencies, principal of my own agency, salesman, marketing consultant, businessman, concert promoter, sales trainer, documentary filmmaker and writer. I've traveled extensively and visited some special countries more than once.

Whether you think you need it or not, approval or validation of your efforts in any endeavor can be important. It sometimes comes in strange ways. Questions still exist about our purpose, goals and accomplishments in Vietnam. If the war remains veiled in a fog for the American public those of us who went and fought are resolute, we did everything right. We did what was asked of us.

I was doing a film for the History Channel titled "Personal Experience, Helicopter Warfare in Vietnam." Easiest and at once, the toughest film I have ever made. I was with my film crew at Fort Rucker, Alabama. Film crews pride themselves on wearing really ratty clothes. It's like a daily competition among them. Holes in their jeans and truly well-worn tee-shirts are de rigueur.

I was dressed comfortably, with long hair, a beard and flip flops. Not directly competing with the guys but comfortable. You get the idea. My crew was crawling all over a very cool, multi-million-dollar Apache helicopter getting shots of everything we were allowed as the training battalion commander walked up.

Captain Saul was frosty. I felt definite icing conditions. He had been ordered to help me with the film and reluctantly, he would. As he asked how he could help, his back was to the final approach of the training field behind him. I noticed over his shoulder an Apache on short final. It was stair-stepping, an unsteady hobby horse flight rather than the normal steady straight line with constant slowing to touch down. I told him it looked like a bird was in trouble behind him.

He turned looked and said, "No, he's just under the bag"

meaning he was on instruments. The captain then said, "Why did you think he was in trouble?"

I said, "Well, I trained here myself a few years back." And it was suddenly like he wanted to start over. As he straightened himself, it looked like he might even reintroduce himself. "Vietnam?" he asked.

"Two tours. Hueys," I replied.

Then he asked with sincerity, "Mr. Jellerson, how can I help you?"

"Well, I'd love to film the Apache at work on the firing range, but the Public Affairs Officer said I can't."

"Really?" he said. "Can your guys be at the range around two today?"

"Yes, we can, Captain."

"Give me a minute." And he walked over to the Colonel PAO who outranked him and said, "I just invited Mr. Jellerson and his film crew to the firing range this afternoon… I'll bet you have a lot of phone calls to make, sir."

That afternoon we set up on the helipad next to his Apache's pad. He pulled the aircraft up to a thirty-foot hover and started firing. The brass from the fifty caliber rounds tinkled down from his aircraft so close we could hear them landing randomly on the concrete pad. Then he fired off two of his Hellfire missiles. Awesome.

But then, the most amazing thing … he cocked the aircraft at about a 45-degree angle and gave the controls to his student in the front seat. From that cockpit he looked down and gave me a snappy salute. As a validation of my service, that was the most important salute I've ever had. I hope Captain Saul survived his service.

One of the most heartbreaking stories I came across never made the final cut.

I interviewed some pilots for the film at Fort Rucker. Came across a pilot who flew Chinooks in Vietnam. He signed my release giving permission to film him and began telling us about one particular mission he flew.

The Chinook is the Army's big twin rotor cargo aircraft. He had flown thirty brand new infantry troops fresh out of basic training to a remote fire support base. The soldiers marched gallantly off the bird in their pressed khakis. The local troops began to put his return load on.

The little base had just been through a grueling assault. His return cargo was exactly thirty body bags filled with thirty dead American troops.

That was all we got out of him. The History Channel film was shot in 2000 and aired in 2001. So, it had been around thirty years since he flew that mission. But the recollection was so fresh in his mind it could have happened only a moment ago. It stopped him, choked him up. He didn't make a sound just closed his eyes tight and started to quietly cry.

Didn't look like he would stop and after a bit it felt an uncomfortable intrusion to stay and watch him in the grip of his hellish memory. We left.

A friend I made on my first documentary film, Tom Lasser, has given me two good ideas for films. We met when I filmed "Personal Experience, Helicopter Warfare in Vietnam." That film now airs on TUBItv, Amazon, and others.

Tom, an Army helicopter pilot and Base Commander of Los Alamitos Army Airfield at the time, was an interviewee for that film. Out of the many hours of raw footage we shot he made the final cut of 93½ minutes. Turned out to be a great friend ever since the shoot.

Tom's first idea was for a documentary about the history of the National Guard. It became a mission for both Tom, another retired colonel, Bill Fortier and me. And it almost happened. We came close in meetings with the Guard's top cadre in the spring of 2020. All agreed on the approach and budget.

Then came the pandemic. And the Guard, as they always are, was called up to assist in this natural disaster. After that, the Guard was activated in many areas because of protests. And the film slid into everyone's rear view mirror.

It's a shame as the Guard's story is really the story of America beginning with the "Minute Men" in 1636. Since their inception, the Guard has been involved in every American war, conflict, police

Home...

action and natural disaster offering aid to those in need. The history of the National Guard is the story of America.

The next validation by another warrior came more subtly.

I was having lunch with Tom one day and he told me about an interesting completely American story and a good idea for a film. He said that if either of us had been shot down in Vietnam and were MIA, they would still be looking for us. The genesis of "A Solemn Promise, America's Missing in Action" was born, also now on TUBI, Amazon and more.

Our nation has over 81,000 MIAs. Incredible in itself. But the most powerful story element is that, proudly, our country never stops looking for them, ever.

Through some help from the Department of Defense I learned of a yearly reunion of the survivors of the Battle of Kham Duc.

I knew in the early stages of the film everyone would understand that when a plane goes missing or a Navy vessel does not come back from a mission there are obviously MIAs. But how in hand-to-hand combat, face to face with the enemy could there be any infantry MIAs? Kham Duc was the most horrific battle of the Vietnam War. It lasted only two days but with hundreds killed on both sides and 31 of ours Missing In Action.

Bill Wright was awarded the Silver Star for his heroism at that battle. I had just met Bill and we were having dinner in an excellent hotel in Oklahoma. I was having my usual aged, single malt scotch with dinner and Bill and I were talking easily. We were just getting to know each other when a second scotch appeared. The waiter said it came from, "Those gentlemen at the bar." At the bar there were three guys my age. Bill told me they were also with the reunion. I waved my thanks but kept my seat.

Soon two more scotches showed up for me. I hadn't even finished my first.

I was determined to do two things. Try to be the good guest my mom raised me to be by finishing all four scotches. And find out what's behind the gesture. So, I excused myself and went to the bar.

My War with Vietnam

One of the guys said, "I know you're here to film Bill, but he tells me you were an Army helicopter pilot."

I said, "Yes I was, but why the drinks?" The vocal one says, "Because you were an Army helicopter pilot in Viet Nam."

"Well thanks, but I wasn't at your battle," I replied. The vocal one goes on, "Doesn't matter. For what you guys did over there for us on the ground there's never going to be an Army pilot within a hundred miles of me that will ever have to buy his own drinks. Thank you."

It was another rewarding validation and a kind of flashback to that incredible bond we shared in combat. I'm proud to be a part of it but membership in that club has a price.

After thorough research of the little-known fact of our 81,000 MIAs I started the journey. Bill Fortier suggested I organize a Film Advisory Committee. These astute, accomplished gentlemen were a measure of how important we all felt this story was. I'm proud to show all of their names in the closing credits of the film.

At a studio one day I was looking for stock footage and came across a scene that still to this day angers me instantly. People ask how I persevered through the long road to getting that film done? It was partly because of my tremendous advisory board cheering me on.

But it was also because of this one scene. Late at night when doubts about my sanity and financial commitment to this project crowded my thoughts, I would play this scene. It appears at 4 min 40 sec in the final cut.

The scene is of a military cemetery gravesite. It's the dead of winter. Trees are bare. People are wearing heavy coats. A young woman is in a chair ten feet or so from a flag-draped coffin. She is sobbing in her grief and the connection is made that it is her young husband in the coffin.

An Army officer in his formal dress blue uniform is handing the woman a folded American flag. This is part of the traditional military ceremony for our fallen warriors. The officer hands her the flag and says to her, "With the thanks of a grateful nation...." As he does so, the camera pulls back.

Home...

And this new widow with her heart breaking in this bitter cold cemetery ... is completely alone.

The twenty or so chairs next to her are empty. What seems a professional mourner is cued to enter the scene. Watching this scene unfold I still get angry at the emptiness of the words, "Thanks of a grateful nation."

Where are they? Where were we? Every goddamned American for a hundred miles should have been there at her side. Should be there en masse every time one of our service men or women dies for this country. Still ashamed and furious she had to be in that cold cemetery alone.

I hope the film might bring this issue to America's awareness.

Wars demand a great deal of healing. I came home through several countries to begin my healing. And I'm apparently still a work in progress.

But these American MIAs are still missing. Still out there somewhere waiting to be found. Their families, as you can well imagine, can't heal either for a lack of closure.

Proudly, we as a nation promise we never leave anyone behind.

America has promised its military, their families and all citizens we will search forever for these fallen warriors. The arm of the government responsible for these searches is the Defense POW/MIA Accounting Agency (DPAA).

As a bureaucracy it is often mired down in excessive paperwork and political roadblocks while dealing with the many countries around the world where these often-hazardous searches must take place. Still their teams work 24/7 to help keep the promise made by our country to those of us our country puts in harm's way.

Perhaps we can all heal, find solace and a substantial deserved pride in this honorable search for our MIAs. That is my heartfelt hope.

I had missed two Christmases and two birthdays while I was away. All but the first birthday passed without notice. Just another day of flying. But that first birthday happened while I was in the 116th. My mom had baked a cake for me and sent it weeks in advance to be safe. Still the mail being what it was the cake arrived weeks after my birthday so, a couple months in the mail.

When I opened it, it was rock hard, actually a chocolate brick. The pilots in my platoon always shared whatever food sent us from home, cookies, brownies, whatever. So, I shared.

It went something like this.... We would literally hatchet off a chunk of chocolate brick. We would put it on a metal plate-tray from the mess hall then soak it in either Schlitz or Blatz beer to soften it up. Hard to express the yummy factor. Surprised the ice cream manufacturers haven't by now tried to duplicate this truly arresting flavor. Thanks Mom.

I saw combat and the world. I can't quantify the reparations I realized through Pan Am Flight One. I am certain that had I gone straight home with all the baggage and horror of war fresh in my mind and heart I would be the lesser for it. I would have started my life over in America, still the monster.

Meeting people all around the planet, being embraced by them, welcomed back to a caring, giving tribe had somehow begun to restore my faith in humanity. I had regained some hope for us all. It was cathartic, therapeutic, healthy.

Not sure yet if it was enough.

Outwardly I must appear to be just outside the norm. To some, I'm sure I appear dysfunctional. I have taken too many chances in my business life.

Not enough in my personal life. Sometimes I feel I've missed something.

I know I've missed some things. And gained much too, though.

I don't know if things would have worked out differently if I hadn't gone to Vietnam. I'll never know. I didn't really expect to sustain that adrenaline rush longer than the year and a half it lasted anyway.

So, I'm healed, all better. But it's the 4th of July and I just left a wonderful party with good friends across the lake where I live. Left before the fireworks started.

Love this country but I hate the 4th of July. Hate fireworks.

Instantly takes me back to a specific mission.

Home...

Back in the 116th I was flying an empty slick behind our gunship lead for a prisoner pick up. Infantry we dropped earlier had taken captives and they would be interrogated. I was about a couple hundred feet behind the lead gunship. Guns two and three were behind me to my right and left. We were doing at least a hundred miles an hour three to four feet off the deck.

Suddenly gunship lead took fire from somewhere in the trees on the left. The pilot on the controls must have been hit and the ship flew directly into the ground. As I said earlier, downed Hueys blow up three times. I banked hard right but flew through the first explosion: fuel. Yellow flames, black smoke instantly on impact.

Close enough to feel the heat I banked around hard again left to see if there were survivors. One of the two remaining gunships escorting me circled too. The other unleashed a salvo of rockets at the tree line. They wouldn't stop to help. Their mission was to fly and kill.

I could stop and land for survivors if there were any.

The second explosion was magnesium parts of the transmission burning white hot. The third explosion is ammunition, rounds cooking off. As a gunship it had mortars, rockets, grenades and machine gun ammunition. Next time you see a fireworks display you'll see what I saw that day. Random, arbitrary explosions of different sizes and projectiles of different breathtaking colors. No survivors.

Amazing I had to leave the party early but still feel I'm healthy and healed.

I'm a positive person and optimistic about the future. The only dream I know I can't fulfill is being happily married to my high school sweetheart for the last fifty years.

Other than that, looking back, about all I missed was a safe, slow transition from childhood to manhood.

Glossary

Arty—Artillery

A.O.—Area of Operation

Ass and Trash—Non-combat, passenger and cargo mission

Break break—Used to separate two radio messages to two parties on the same frequency

Concertina wire—Barbed wire with embedded razors

Cambode—Slang for Cambodia

C.O.—Commanding Officer

Chalk two, Etc.—Positions in formation flying

C.B.s—Construction Battalion

Di Di (Dee Dee)—Vietnamese verb for leave or exit

Daisy Chain—Gunship maneuver for constant coverage of a target. Three gunships fly in attacking their target using opposite circular orbits with turns alternating to left then right. Allows for constant fire power over the target. Viewed from above, this looks like petals on a flower.

D.F.C.—Distinguished Flying Cross

Eagle flight—Small, three to six ship formations as opposed to full infantry company insertions of nine ships or more

Flaming Mimis—Shot of bourbon set afire; drinking it "proves mettle" of new pilots

Freq—Radio frequency (also "push")

Grunt—Infantry soldier

Guard frequency—Overrides all freqs so pilots can listen exclusively for "May days"

Glossary

Grape Smoke—Purple smoke

Hooch—Primitive living quarters

Klick—One kilometer

Lemon Smoke—Yellow smoke

L.Z.—Landing Zone

Mikes—Minutes

Mini-guns—7.62 caliber Gatling gun fires 3000–6000 rounds per minute

M.P.—Military Police

O-Club—Officer's Club

Peter Pilot—Newbie Copilot

P.O.L. Dump—Petroleum, oil, lubricant (gas station)

Pax—Passengers

Push—Radio frequency

Pop smoke—Colored smoke canisters released to identify friendly positions and wind direction and speed

Rescap—Rescue cover or "cap"

R.T.O.—Radio Telephone Operator

R & R—Rest and Recreation

R.V.N.—Republic of Viet Nam

"Puff the Magic Dragon" C-47 twin engine cargo plane converted to gunship with 3 miniguns on left side. Flies in left hand orbit over target.

"Spooky"—AC-130 Gunship, six plus mini-guns (larger "Puff")

Spider Hole—Cave or burrow with turf/foliage cover or lid for hiding enemy.

Slick—Lightly armed Hueys for troop carrying/Medevac/cargo etc.

S.O.L.—Shit outa luck

Sortie—Aviation speak for a single mission

N.V.A.—North Vietnamese Army Regulars

V.C.—Viet Cong (Communist guerrilla) (Victor Charlie)

Index

ABC *Night of Champions* 12
ABC Television 10, 12, 15, 22, 37, 42, 55, 62, 123, 173
Against the Odds 32, 73
Akron Beacon Journal 78
Aladdin Hotel, Las Vegas, NV 27
Albert, Marv 112
Ali, Muhammad 3, 9–10, 12, 14, 17, 18, 20–24, 29, 32, 38, 46, 47, 51–52, 54, 67, 82, 92, 105, 109, 122–123, 128, 134, 137, 150, 156, 174, 181–183, 210
American Medical Association 167
Andreoli, Bob 73
Apartheid 2, 5, 29, 79. 96–97, 106, 156
Arcel, Ray 50, 108, 172
Arguello, Alexis 73
Artists and Athletes Against Apartheid 96–97
Arum, Bob 12–13, 17, 29–30, 39, 41, 60, 96–97, 141, 165
Ashe, Arthur 97
Atlantic City 2, 73, 169, 173, 177, 180, 183–185, 191–192, 203–204
Atlantic City Convention Hall 196
Atlas, Teddy 6, 194
Ayala, Tony 157, 177

Baer, Buddy 108–109
Baer, Max 109
Baker, Lena 9–10
Barkley, Iran 203
Barry, Dave 96
Benton, George 53, 80, 178–179
Berbick, Trevor 27, 32–35, 37, 46, 52–53, 56, 85, 97, 116, 122, 126–130, 144–149, 156, 160–161, 200, 204
Berger, Phil 62, 73
Bernstein, Al 41
Bey, David 45, 90, 94, 97, 101–104, 109, 128, 178–179
Bey, Joseph 101
Biggs, Tyrell 95, 157, 176–181
Blackburn, Jack 108

Bobick, Duane 5, 13, 16
Borges, Ron 204–205
Boston Globe 94, 103, 119, 127, 130, 167, 205
Bounds, Kenny 91
Bowe, Riddick 209
Boyle's Thirty Acres, Jersey City, NJ 73
Braddock, James J. 141–142, 148, 151, 182
Branchini, Umberto 10
Bright, Jay 199, 205
British Boxing Board of Control 137, 201
Broad, James 80, 92, 107, 157, 166, 174
Brown, Drew "Bundini" 9, 25, 110
Brown, Phil 118
Brunette, Frank 133
Bruno, Frank 2, 92, 127, 136–141, 159, 185, 196, 199, 200–204, 210–211
Bruton, Mike 100
Buffalo Memorial Auditorium, Buffalo, NY 105
Bugner, Joe 80, 201
Bynam, Arlen 129

Caesars Palace, Las Vegas, NV 11, 21, 23, 34, 44, 50, 56–57, 80, 121
Caesars Palace Sports Pavilion, Las Vegas, NV 34, 56
Cannon, Jimmy 3
Canter, George 62
Cappuccino, Frank 172, 196
Carnera, Primo 124
Carpenter, Harry 203
Carpentier, George 61, 73
Cavanaugh, Jack 121
Cayton, Bill 192, 196–197, 199–200, 205
Chaplin, George 44, 57
Charles, Ezzard 43, 110
Cecchini, Harry 125
Chicago 40, 46, 96, 142
Chicago Tribune 103
Chisora, Derek 209
Cobb, Randall "Tex" 35, 44–45, 53–57, 61, 63, 68, 166

Index

Coetzee, Gerrie 5, 28–30, 42, 44, 56, 72, 76–79, 82–83, 86–87, 90–91, 96–99, 101–102, 104–105, 127, 138, 210
Cohen, Marty 78
Collins, Nigel 36, 148, 172, 186
Convention Centre, Las Vegas, NV 85
Cooney, Gerry 2, 28, 30, 35, 38–40, 42–45, 47–55, 62, 68, 72, 79, 94, 101, 127, 134–135, 145, 149, 151, 155–157, 164–165, 169, 170–174
Cooney, Tony 47
Cortez, Joe 133, 186–187
Cosell, Howard 10, 11, 16, 17, 21, 22, 25, 38, 55, 164
Cowen, Jack 142
Cummings, Floyd "Jumbo" 46, 138–139, 142
Curtis, Joey 58–59, 64–65
Cushman, Tom 10, 20
Cuthbert, GA 9–10

D'Amato, Cus 6, 95, 130, 149, 164, 185, 191, 194, 198, 200
Damiani, Francesco 2
Dempsey, Jack 19, 61, 73, 96, 121, 148, 158, 172, 180
Dixon, Tris 137
Dokes, Michael 27, 35, 38–39, 44, 53, 55–59, 61, 63–67, 72, 76–79, 88, 98, 114, 208
Donald, Larry 210
Donovan, Arthur 108
Douglas, Billy "Dynamite" 165
Douglas, James "Buster" 1, 126, 165, 166, 169, 174, 200, 204, 208, 211
Downey, Mike 119
Duff, Mickey 91, 138
Dundee, Angelo 25, 40–41, 67, 69, 88–89, 100, 115, 127–129, 146, 149, 161, 163–164
Dunes Hotel and Casino, Las Vegas, NV 63, 67
Du Plooy, Johnny 2
Dupree, Rodell 61
Duran, Roberto 45, 55, 72, 104, 157, 203
Duva, Lou 178

Ecklund, Anders 138, 142
Edmerson, Leroy 85
Elbaum, Don 105
Ellis, Jimmy 123
Empire State Convention Centre, Albany, NY 96
Evangelista, Alfredo 4, 10, 21, 36, 38, 61, 79, 142

Ferguson, Jesse 130, 158, 166, 206
Ferrera, Robert 125

Ferringo, Lou 189
Fire and Fear: The Inside Story Of Mike Tyson 207
Fischer, Tom 27
Fitzgerald, Ed 19
Fitzsimmons, Bob 92, 137
Ford, Duane 89, 134
Foreman, George 3–4, 23, 25, 118, 190, 192, 198
Foster, Bob 116
Frank, Scott 73–75, 79, 82, 84
Frazier, Joe 25, 33, 46, 73, 75, 80, 81, 82, 116, 182
Frazier, Marvis 2, 73, 75, 79, 80, 81, 82, 84, 153, 158
Fury, Tyson 209
Futch, Eddie 33–34, 37–38, 50–51, 63, 67, 70, 74–75, 80, 100, 111, 117, 120, 128–130, 133, 143, 146, 171, 175, 183, 193–194

Gardner, Chuck 201
Gardner, John L. 38
Garrett, Sam 3
Giachetti, Richie 5, 10, 33, 37, 117, 119–120, 131, 133, 184–185, 188–190
Giardello, Joey 110
Gibbs, Harry 148
Givens, Robin 164, 175, 190, 192, 199, 207
Givens, Stephanie 192
Goldman, Herbert 80
Golota, Andrew 210
Gomez, Wilfredo 11
Gordon, Randy 47
Gordon, S.T. 128, 146
Gould, Joe 142
Graham, Bill 177
Graziano, Carmine 110–111, 206
Green, Dave "Boy" 12
Green, Mitch 128, 152, 154, 199
Greer, Thom 48, 71
Gregg, Eddie 127, 135
Griffith, Emile 157
Griffith Stadium, Washington, DC 108
Grimsley, Will 18, 48
Gross, Reggie 201
The Guardian 138
Guerra, Jose 159

Hadley, Odell 190–191
Hagler, Marvelous Marvin 4, 39, 40, 72, 104, 118, 162
Hamsho, Mustapha 40
Harrah's Marina Hotel Casino, Atlantic City, NJ 74
Hart, Colin 202
Hart, Marvin 165
Hassett, Chuck 70

Index

Hauser, Thomas 22, 26
Hayes, Isaac 125
Hazzard, Larry 65
Hearns, Thomas 11, 72, 104
Heeney, Tom 19
Hernandez, Ferd 27
Hilton Hotel, Las Vegas, NV 130, 133, 143–145, 148, 156, 160, 173, 176, 199, 203, 211
Hoffer, Richard 87, 103
Hoffman, Ancil 108
Holmes, Diane 70–71, 109
Holmes, Larry 1–6, 18–19, 30, 32, 35, 39–40, 46, 56–57, 72, 76, 78, 84–89, 98–99, 103–105, 107, 114–116; vs. Ali 22–28; vs. Berbick 32–35; vs. Bey 99–103; vs. Cobb 53–56; vs. Cooney 47–52; vs. Frank 73–75; vs. Frazier 79–83; vs. Jones 12–17; vs. Le Doux 19–22; vs. Rodriguez 60–63; vs. Smith 90–94; vs. Snipes 41–44; vs. Spinks, Leon 36–38; vs. Spinks, Michael (1st fight) 116–121; vs. Spinks, Michael (2nd fight) 130–135; vs. Tyson 183–188; vs. Williams 109–113; vs. Witherspoon 67–71; vs. Zanon 9–12
Holyfield, Evander 95, 136–137, 189, 205, 208–209, 211
Home Box Office (HBO) 4, 33–34, 40, 46, 50–51, 77, 84, 89, 92–93, 102, 115, 118–119, 122, 125–127, 129–130, 135, 139–141, 143–146, 148–149, 152, 155, 158–160, 173, 177–178, 180, 185–186, 190, 193, 195–196, 200, 203
Honda, Akihiko 188
Honeyghan, Lloyd 91
Horne, John 200
Houston Astrodome, TX 54
Hunter, Jim 86

In the Cheap Seats 198
International Boxing Federation (IBF) 2, 6, 85–87, 90–92, 99–101, 109–110, 113, 116–117, 120, 122, 127, 130, 132–133, 135–136, 141, 143–144, 147, 155–157, 160, 164–169, 173–174, 176–177, 183, 188, 191, 193, 195, 199, 207
Isaak, Kevin 36
Izenberg, Jerry 51

Jackson, the Rev. Jesse 163
Jackson, Julian 200
Jacobs, Jimmy 141, 146–147, 157, 159, 175, 178–179, 181, 190–191, 197, 200, 205
Jacobs, Lorraine 205
Jacobs, Mike 108
Jameson, Mike 147
Jeffries, James J. 9, 25, 111, 165, 168–169, 183
Joe Louis Arena, Detroit, MI 37

Johansson, Ingemar 142
Johnson, Jack 9, 25, 52, 66, 111, 134, 168
Johnson, Jim 66
Johnson, John 208
Johnson, Marvin 12, 144
Jones, Leroy 11–17, 21
Jones, Mike 47, 52
Joshua, Anthony 209
Jowett, J.R. 106

Katz, Michael 38, 119, 144, 146, 149, 152, 157, 167, 179, 195, 201, 204
Keating, Frank 138
Kerzner, Sol 97
Kim, Deuk Koo 58–60
King, Carl 57, 59, 68, 88, 124, 141, 152, 200
King, Don 1, 3, 11–12, 17, 21, 23, 26–27, 31, 33, 42–44, 49, 52, 54, 56–57, 59–63, 68, 73, 77–78, 83, 85, 87–88, 90, 96–97, 100, 104–105, 107, 113, 115–116, 119, 124–128, 130, 132, 135, 141, 145, 152–154, 159, 160, 165, 180, 192, 199, 201–202, 205, 208
Knight, Ernest 9–10
Knoetze, Kallie 5
KO magazine 159, 196
Koranicki, Mike 29
Kornberg, Alan 92, 157
Kushner, Cedric 97, 165

Lampley, Jim 173, 190, 196, 203
Lane, Mills 51, 82, 113, 148–149, 167, 176–177
Las Vegas, NV 2, 9, 10, 12, 21–23, 27, 32–33, 47, 50, 56–57, 63–64, 67, 73, 79, 83–85, 87, 90, 92, 99–00, 103, 113, 116, 127–128, 130, 141, 143–145, 155–156, 160, 162, 164, 166, 173, 183, 185, 199, 202, 211
Lawless, Terry 138, 202
Lawlor Events Centre, Reno, NV 111
Layne, Rex 32
Lederman, Harold 65, 120, 129, 140, 159
LeDoux, Scott 17, 19–22
Lee, Jeong-Sook 127
Leonard, Sugar Ray 12, 51, 93, 104, 162, 170
Lewis, Butch 103, 113, 118–119, 122, 130–132, 135, 141, 142, 149, 155–156, 168–169, 172–173, 177, 194, 196
Lewis, Lennox 209
The Life and Crimes of Don King: The Shame of Boxing in America 3, 33, 96, 141
Liston, Sonny 10, 25, 88, 92, 150, 198
Logan, Greg 112, 135, 193
London, Brian 137
Los Angeles Times 48, 55, 87, 103, 119, 121, 201, 211
Louis, Joe 37, 92, 101, 108–109, 119, 134, 142, 147, 151, 182–183, 193

Index

Lupica, Mike 24, 48, 50
Lurie, Art 129
Lyle, Ron 20, 47–49
Lyon, Bill 64, 70, 80, 131, 135, 143

Madison Square Garden, New York, NY 2, 4, 19, 32, 48, 96, 108, 151, 157, 172, 182
Mancini, Ray 58, 72
Manuel, Don 13, 59
Marantz, Steve 94, 103, 119, 127, 130, 167
Marciano, Peter 121
Marciano, Rocky 2, 32, 40, 54, 91, 94, 109–110, 116–117, 121, 134–135, 148, 150, 158, 168, 207
Mathis, Buster 189
Matthews, Wallace 120, 123, 127, 132, 134, 138, 164, 170, 194
Mayo Clinic, Rochester, MN 22
McCall, Oliver 208
McIlvanney, Hugh 46
McRae, Donald 3
Melody, Tom 78
Mercado, Bernardo 27, 33, 36, 45, 53
Mercante, Arthur 191
Mercedes, Hector 96
Mercer, Ray 210
Merchant, Larry 33–34, 51, 82, 84–86, 92, 102, 119–120, 125, 129, 135, 158–160, 167, 181, 186, 196, 204, 207
Metropolitan Sports Centre, Bloomington, MN 20
Miller, Hal 89
Miller, Norm 17
Minker, Chuck 70, 85
Monroe, Marty 20, 35
Moore, Archie 69, 117, 150
Moretti, Dave 120, 148
Morton, Janks 97
Mouzon, Wesley 137
Mugabi, John 157
Muhammad, Eddie Mustapha 13, 42
Muhammad, Herbert 25–26
Muhammad, Murad 73, 111
Murray, Jim 55, 201, 211

Nagler, Barney 18
Nelson, Steve 92
Neumann, Randy 207
Nevada State Athletic Commission 22, 24, 59, 131, 134
New Orleans Superdome 13
New York Daily News 44, 48, 50, 55, 63, 82, 94, 119, 126, 144, 146, 149, 157, 167, 179, 191, 201
New York State Athletic Commission 151–152, 155
New York Times 38

Newfield, Jack 3, 25, 33, 96, 141
Newman, Phil 177
Newsday 112, 120, 123, 127, 134–135, 138, 164, 170, 193–194
Norton, Ken 4, 10, 19–20, 34–35, 39, 48–49, 53, 69, 100, 113, 122, 183

The Observer 46
Ocasio, Ossie 4, 21, 57
Omni Arena, Atlanta, GA 123, 125
Orlando, Tony 181
Ortega, Rudy 41, 43, 148

Pacheco, Dr Ferdie 12, 22, 24, 54, 74, 111
Padilla, Carlos 163
Page, Greg 35, 38–39, 44, 52, 55–56, 71–73, 79, 82–86, 88, 90–91, 97–99, 101–102, 104–107, 123–124, 126, 128, 136, 146–147, 166, 168
Parkinson, Michael 26
Patterson, Floyd 79, 95, 142, 150
Pearl, Davey 20, 93, 145
Pepe, Phil 55, 63, 94
Perez, Tony 75, 77, 78
Philadelphia Daily News 10, 109, 124, 158, 188, 200
Pittsburgh Press 45
Press and Sun Bulletin (Binghamton, New York) 21
Prezant, Bill 127
Price, Lloyd 3
Pryor, Aaron 72–73
Putnam, Pat 23

Qawi, Dwight Muhammad 136–137
Quarry, Jerry 10, 123

Rademacher, Pete 79
Rappaport, Dennis 47–49, 52, 174
Ratliff, Alfonzo 142, 144–145
Rattenni, Nick 41
Reagan, Ronald 121
Reno, NV 27, 58, 86, 109, 111, 164
Reno Gazette-Journal 164
Reuters 121
Ribalta, Jose 158, 208
Richard, Dennis 152–153
Richfield Coliseum, Richfield, OH 76
The Ring 2, 15–16, 18, 28, 38, 41, 47–48, 63–64, 70, 72, 79, 86, 92, 106, 141, 148, 170, 172–173, 186, 195, 210
Rivera, Luis 154
Riviera Hotel and Casino, Las Vegas, NV 88, 91, 100, 113, 116, 127
Robinson, "Slim" Jim 68, 125
Rocky 47
Rocky 2 47

192

Index

Rocky 3 47
Rodda, John 138
Rodrigues, Adilson 205
Rodriguez, Isidro 99
Rodriguez, Lucien 60, 63–67, 68, 70, 142
Roldan, Julio 177
Roman, Joe 190
Romero, Dr. Ronald 59
Rooney, Kevin 147, 162, 163, 175, 194, 199, 205
Root, Jack 165
Roper, Ruth 192
Rossman, Mike 110
Roth, Jerry 65, 85, 133
Ryan, Jeff 159

Santos, Herb 70
Sauter, Van Gordon 29
Schmeling, Max 151, 182–183
Schulian, John 26
Scroggins, John 16
Sesquicentennial Stadium, Philadelphia, PA 19
Shavers, Earnie 4–5, 10, 17–18, 21, 27, 53, 56, 92, 187
Shilstone, Mackie 117, 119
Shirley, Dalby 89, 159
Simms, Jeff 12, 178
Smith, Elmer 109, 124, 158, 188, 200, 204
Smith, Harold 189
Smith, James "Bonecrusher" 91–92, 100, 105, 110, 116, 138–139, 151–159, 161–162, 184, 201, 203
Smith, Paul 129
Sneddon, Steve 164
Snipes, Renaldo 41, 42, 43, 44, 64, 67, 71, 72, 73, 79, 128, 146, 178, 179
Snowell, Aaron 199, 205
Soldier Field, Chicago, IL 96
Solis, Ray 11
South African Boxing Board of Control 99
Spinelli, Joe 32–33
Spinks, Leon 3, 12, 21, 27–28, 34–39, 51, 54, 93, 104, 109, 116, 118, 122, 144, 156, 162, 174, 183, 194, 210
Spinks, Michael 2, 72, 94, 103, 109, 113, 116, 118–119, 122–123, 127, 130, 132–133, 136, 141, 144, 147, 149, 155, 160, 165, 169–170, 173–174, 176–177, 181–185, 191, 193–194, 196, 198, 206, 210
Sports Illustrated 65
Steele, Richard 38, 89, 143, 203
Stein, Gary 21
Stevenson, Teofilo 5
Stewart, Alex 137
Stewart, Bobby 6

Sugar, Bert 38
Sulaiman, Jose 60, 83, 156
The Sun 202
Sun City Superbowl, Sun City, South Africa 98
Swart, Phil 99

Tabat, Lou 159
Tangstad, Steffen 141–144, 165
Tate, John 5, 11–17, 27–29, 33, 40, 52, 76, 83, 86, 91, 98, 114, 128, 210
Tennison, Ray 59
Terrell, Ernie 54, 142
Thomas, Cathy 87
Thomas, Duane 157
Thomas, Pinklon 76, 87–90, 107, 113–116, 121–124, 126–128, 130, 139, 146–147, 157, 160–161, 167, 174, 210
Tillis, James 39, 40, 41, 56, 57, 79, 87, 110, 112, 201, 206
Tillman, Henry 95, 196
Tocco, Johnny 202
Tokyo Dome, Tokyo, Japan 190
Toledo, Springs 198
Tompkins, Barry 34, 50, 89, 148, 190
Torres, Jose 145, 153, 155, 207
Trump, Donald 169, 173, 185, 193
Trump Plaza Hotel and Casino, Atlantic City, NJ 169, 173, 185–186
Tubbs, Tony 2, 104–106, 122–127, 136–137, 147, 152–155, 165, 187–189, 190–191, 193, 210
Tucker, Hal 29, 99
Tucker, Robert 174
Tucker, Tony 155, 160, 164–167, 169, 173–177, 182, 185, 210
Tunney, Gene 19, 96, 121 168–169
Tyson, Mike 1–3, 6–7, 95–96, 123, 127, 130, 141, 143–145, 150–151, 153–155, 165–167, 169–170, 173, 182, 198–199, 209–211; vs. Berbick 145–149; vs. Biggs 177–181; vs. Bruno 199–204; vs. Holmes 183–187; vs. Smith 155–160; vs. Spinks, Michael 191–197; vs. Thomas 160–164; vs. Tubbs 188–191; vs. Tucker 173–177; vs. Williams 204–208

Valle, Victor 50–51
Verdi, Bob 103
Verigan, Bill 126

Walcott, Jersey Joe 43, 110, 147–148
Wallace, Lawrence 120
Ward, Stan 76
Washington, Desiree 211
Waters, Bob 47
Watres Armory, Scranton, PA 62

Index

Weaver, Mike 4–5, 10–18, 20–21, 27–31, 33, 35, 39–41, 48–49, 53, 56–59, 63–66, 72, 76–77, 87–88, 92, 98, 113–115, 127, 153, 157, 160–161, 206, 210
Wembley Stadium, London, UK 2, 137, 199
West, Joe 87
Wevurski, Pete 45
Wiley, Ralph 65
Willard, Jess 124, 148, 172
Williams, Carl 1, 109–113, 204–207
Williams, Dr. Charles 23
Williams, Cleveland 25
Witherspoon, Anthony 175
Witherspoon, Tim 2, 61–63, 67–74, 79, 84–90, 94, 97, 104, 107, 114, 116, 122–128, 136–141, 147, 151–155, 157, 161, 188–189, 201–202, 209–210
Woods, Edward 125
World Boxing Association (WBA) 2, 5–6, 11–13, 15, 17, 28–29, 39–40, 47, 52–53, 56–57, 60, 63–67, 72, 76–77, 79, 82–83, 86–87, 91, 94, 96–99, 101–102, 104–106, 114, 122–123, 125–127, 136–141, 144, 147, 151–155, 158, 160, 162, 170, 173, 175–177, 183, 188, 191, 199, 201, 204–205, 207, 210
World Boxing Council (WBC) 1–2, 4–6, 9–12, 16, 19–22, 24, 26–28, 30, 32, 36, 39, 41–42, 47, 49, 53, 56–57, 60–61, 63–64, 67–68, 71, 73–74, 76, 78–79, 81–84, 86–87, 90, 94, 104, 107, 113–114, 121–124, 126–129, 138, 144–146, 149–150, 155–156, 158, 160, 162, 168, 170, 173, 175–177, 183, 188, 191, 199, 201, 204–205, 210
World Boxing Organization (WBO) 2

Yoda 5
Young, Dick 44, 46, 48, 131
Young, Jimmy 45, 47, 57

Zanon, Lorenzo 1, 9, 10, 11, 21

www.ingramcontent.com/pod-product-compliance
Ingram Content Group UK Ltd.
Pitfield, Milton Keynes, MK11 3LW, UK
UKHW032020300125
454454UK00015B/197